VIRGINIA WOOLF

VIRGINIA WOOLF

A CRITICAL MEMOIR

WINIFRED HOLTBY

CASSANDRA EDITIONS

ACADEMY
PRESS
LIMITED

CHICAGO

1978

Cassandra Editions 1978
Published by Academy Press Limited
360 North Michigan Avenue, Chicago, Ill. 60601
Printed and bound in the United States of America

CONTENTS

AUTHOR'S NOTE

THE form and scope of this essay require, perhaps, a word of explanation. I began to write it two years ago, but its completion was delayed. Since then Mrs. Woolf has published *The Waves* and *A Letter to a Young Poet*, and a number of uncollected articles, while in France has appeared M. Delattre's important study *Le Roman psychologique de Virginia Woolf*. I have therefore somewhat revised one or two passages in the text to include reference to these, and rewritten the last chapter, though I have retained the main portions of my original monograph.

I should like to make it clear also that I claim no authoritative justification. When I began collecting my material I had seen Mrs. Woolf only twice, at formal and public functions. Once, while I was working on the book, I asked for and obtained one interview, during which, at my request, she supplied me with copies of some of her critical articles which I could not otherwise have obtained without great difficulty, and also confirmed some biographical details which seemed to me desirable for a study of this kind. I am greatly indebted to Dame Ethel Smyth for her invaluable help in reading through and correcting certain of the more personal passages in Chapter I.

But for the facts themselves, and still more for the deductions that I have drawn from them, I alone must accept responsibility. Mrs. Woolf has neither read my manuscript nor authorised any statement made in it. Her sole instruction was that I should treat her work with the candour and impartiality applied by critics to the writings of the dead. If, in attempting to fulfil her mandate, I have too often or too grossly misinterpreted her intention, my consolation is that she still has the remedies of the living, and may defend herself.

I

THE ADVANTAGES OF BEING
VIRGINIA STEPHEN

AT the beginning of Virginia Woolf's second novel, *Night and Day*, is a description of what it feels like to be born the daughter of a distinguished literary family. " The quality of her birth oozed into Katharine's consciousness from a dozen different sources as soon as she was able to perceive anything. Above her nursery fireplace hung a photograph of her grandfather's tomb in Poet's Corner, and she was told in one of those moments of grown-up confidence which are so tremendously impressive to the child's mind, that he was buried there because he was ' a good and great man.' . . . Again and again she was brought down into the drawing-room to receive the blessing of some awful distinguished old man who sat, even to the childish eye, somewhat apart, all gathered together and clutching a stick, unlike an ordinary visitor, in her father's own armchair, and her father himself was there, unlike himself, too, a little excited and very polite. These formidable old creatures used to take her in their arms, look very keenly in her eyes, and then to bless her, and tell her that she must mind and be a good girl. . . . Her earliest conceptions of the world included an august circle of beings to whom she gave the names of Shakespeare, Milton, Words-worth, Shelley, and so on, who were, for some reason, much more nearly akin to the Hilberys than to other people. They made a kind of boundary to her vision of life, and played a considerable part in determining her scale of good and bad in her own small affairs." There is no reason to suppose that this passage is completely autobiographical, but the childhood of the girl who was one day to be Virginia Woolf cannot have been, at least in this particular, so very unlike that of Katharine Hilbery.

She was the daughter of Leslie Stephen, and when she was born her father was editing that epitome of solid and scholarly English journalism, the *Cornhill Magazine*. He had been a Cambridge don, adoring Cambridge, and confessing till the end of his life a complete belief in Cambridge ideals and " an almost superstitious veneration " for a Senior Wrangler. But he sacrificed even Cambridge and the coveted irresponsibility of a deanery to his respect for truth, resigning from his tutorship when he found himself unable to believe whole-heartedly in the Thirty-nine Articles and unwilling to practise the polite deception of conformity, then required of a man in his position. He came to London, and entered that life of a man of letters which well suited his scholarly and fastidious temperament. His subsequent career was of immense distinction. He knew everyone. Browning, Matthew Arnold, Henry Fawcett and Ruskin were among his friends. His brother was the famous Fitzjames Stephen ; Thomas Hardy was one of his early contributors to the *Cornhill*. His own literary output, critical, biographical and philosophical, was enormous ;

but especially was he a biographer. While Virginia was a child he left the *Cornhill* to enter upon the great work with which his name is specially identified, the editorship of the *Dictionary of National Biography*. Sidney Lee was his sub-editor. The work involved was prodigious ; the difficulties great. After planning the whole and completing one-third, Leslie Stephen retired and left the field to his second-in-command. The labour and strain had been too much for him. But he continued himself to publish an impressive series of biographical and critical works, to entertain other scholars and literary men, and to build up one of the finest private collections of eighteenth-century books in England. The experience of being kissed by " awful distinguished old men " must have been a familiar one to his daughters.

His family was complicated. He had married twice, his first wife being a daughter of the great Thackeray, by whom he had one child, an invalid. Then he married a barrister's widow, Mrs. Duckworth, with three children of her own by her first husband, and she eventually became the mother also of Vanessa, Julian Thoby, Virginia and Adrian Stephen. She died when Virginia was only thirteen.

People who remember her to-day always speak first of her beauty. She had been Julia Prinsep Jackson and was half French, and must have been extraordinarily lovely. Mrs. Woolf declares that her mother's family had been " extremely frivolous and art-loving and sociable " compared with her father's, " the Stephens, who were all lawyers, and the Venns, who had been country gentry and clergymen since the time of Elizabeth and before."

In two of Mrs. Woolf's novels, *The Voyage Out* and *To the Lighthouse*, appear portraits of an almost identical couple, although in *The Voyage Out* they are called Helen and Ridley Ambrose, and in *To the Lighthouse* Mr. and Mrs. Ramsay. In each couple, the husband is very learned, very eccentric, with an odd habit of reciting poetry aloud to himself, a *poseur*, self-conscious, absent-minded, touchy, scrupulous, with a queer egotism and queerer nobility ; the wife is beautiful, imperious, maternal, candid, with a sort of vigour and radiance about her. I do not say that these are portraits of Mr. and Mrs. Leslie Stephen, but there must have been some quality about such a couple which burned itself into the consciousness of Virginia Woolf. A novelist does not usually repeat a portrait except for some special reason.

There exists to-day in the British Museum a little book, now out of print, published by Mrs. Stephen in 1883, called *Notes from Sick Rooms*, which is interesting, not only for the sidelights which it casts upon the Stephen family, but for its clear proof that Virginia inherited the instinct to write from her mother as well as from her father. For all its modest and practical pretensions, it is significant also, because, oddly enough, in its homely advice about beds, diet and hygiene, now a trifle outmoded by medical fashion, there are more resemblances to Virginia's later literary style than in all her father's immense catalogue of published works. It shares that peculiar humour, consisting of a mixture of irony and extravagance, which lights up *Orlando* and *A Room of One's Own*. It displays the whimsical hyperbole, the half-amused detachment, the trick of remote and yet illuminating reference, and something of the wondering, contemplative mind inherited by the daughter. Here, for instance, is a characteristic passage about " Crumbs in the Bed." " Among the number of small evils which haunt illness, the greatest, in the misery which it can cause, is crumbs. The origin of most things has been decided on, but the origin of crumbs in bed has never excited sufficient attention among the scientific world, though it is a problem which has tormented many a weary sufferer. I will forbear to give my explanation, which could be neither scientific nor orthodox, and I will merely beg that their evil existence may be recognised and, as far as human nature allows, guarded against. The torment of crumbs should be stamped out of the sick bed as if it were the Colorado beetle in a potato field."

" The origin of most things has been decided on." . . . Is not that an almost perfect Virginia Woolf remark, observing, with characteristic amusement, the absurdities of learned and abstract discussion ? The shadows of St. John Hirst, Charles Tansley, Ridley Ambrose and Mr. Ramsay creep from it across the page. Mrs. Stephen, much occupied with her sensitive, delicate and difficult family, must have had ample opportunity of listening to philosophers determining the origin of most things, yet ignoring completely the possible explanation of crumbs.

Virginia was brought up partly in London, partly in Cornwall. One of the few stories I have heard of her childhood is of a small naked baby being plunged by a tall father in and out of the water on the Cornish coast. The thought of the sea haunts her writing. She never loses an opportunity to send her characters on a voyage, to an island, to the sea-shore. That amazing opening in Cornwall of *Jacob's Room*, the sea holiday of Jacob and Tim Durrant, the whole setting of *To the Lighthouse*, Mrs. Dalloway's feeling of being " out, out, far out to sea and alone," Katharine Hilbery's dream of a lover " riding a great horse by the shore of the sea," the interludes of sea-scape, and, indeed, the entire conception of *The Waves*—all these and a thousand more sea-memories surely come to her from her childhood. When her characters are ill, or suffering from minds deranged, like Rachel Vinrace or Septimus Warren Smith, their imagination sets them under the sea. In *The Mark on the Wall* Mrs. Woolf thinks of a submarine world down among " the gray waters with their sudden gleams of light and their reflections." The sea colours, green and blue, shine through her work, evidently delighting her as white and crimson delighted the Brontës. Even her metaphors assume a maritime quality. No other aspect of natural life seems to have affected her in the same way, except when, after her Richmond period, she wrote of stags—the barking of stags, of ankles like stags, of children stealing like stags from the table, of the stags in Orlando's house. There are, of course, stags on Richmond Park. But the sea was an earlier and profounder influence. Probably the sea, with its power and freedom, affected her more than it might have affected some children, because she was in childhood, as she has always been, extremely delicate, too delicate to go to school or college, or to pass through the usual routine of education. She was probably shy. Her imagination must always have been extraordinarily sensitive. Temperament and circumstances combined to limit her experience. But she loved all that was wild, adventurous and vital. She fell early and completely in love with the Elizabethan Age. She told me that she devoured Hakluyt's *Voyages* with nothing less than passion. Every book that she has written bears evidence of that love. Orlando opens his career as an Elizabethan gallant. *The Voyage Out* leads to a South America described straight out of Raleigh's *Discovery of Guiana*. In *Night and Day* Henry Otway's brow was " arched in the Elizabethan manner, but the gentle honest eyes were sceptical rather than glowing with Elizabethan fervour." The mind of Rachel Vinrace was in " the state of an intelligent man's at the beginning of the reign of Queen Elizabeth." Shakespeare, the possible fate of Shakespeare's sister, the age of Shakespeare, haunt her mind.

All this was important to her development as a writer. If, on the one side, her experience was as restricted and decorous as Jane Austen's, on the other,

her imagination was almost as much sea-haunted as Conrad's. The combination gives its strange effect of wildness and tranquillity to her work.

She cannot, however, have been, like so many writers, a lonely child. She had her sister, Vanessa, who seems to have been a special friend, and when sisters are friends the relationship goes deep to the roots of personality. Vanessa is now Vanessa Bell, the painter, to whom Virginia Woolf dedicated her second novel—" but in looking for a phrase," she adds, " I found none to stand beside your name." She has drawn decorative designs to Virginia's stories. To know a painter intimately is an educational experience for a writer, and Virginia Woolf's work shows that the rule held good for her. She seems to enjoy intro-ducing painters into her novels in order that she may describe them at work—Mrs. Flushing in *The Voyage Out*, Charles Steele in *Jacob's Room*, Lily Briscoe in *To the Lighthouse*. She is at home in the painter's world of form and colour. Her own imagination seems to be visual rather than aural. " The grove has only to be called ἄβατον, ' untrodden,' " she writes, " and we imagine the twisted branches and the purple violets "—a painter's vision.

She had also the companionship of young men and boys—her brothers and half-brothers. Her novels show how well she knew and understood young men. But they are intellectual young men. The talk of sport, motor-cars, machinery and business which occupies so many pages of much contemporary fiction, and still more hours of contemporary life, hardly enters into her work. All her characters write, paint, lecture, teach, edit the classics or study in the British Museum. For a few moments in *The Voyage Out* she creates a shadowy young man interested in aeroplanes ; Peter Walsh in *Mrs. Dalloway* is a man of action rather than a thinker ; Richard Dalloway is a Member of Parliament. But clearly she has always been more familiar with people who use their minds rather than their bodies as their equipment for life. She has never understood the stupid. Whenever she tries to draw a character like Betty Flanders or Mrs. Denham, she loses her way. They are more foreign to her than princes were to Jane Austen. Her imagination falters on the threshold of stupidity.

Though she was unable to endure a regular education, she enjoyed an unusually effective training as a writer. Partly, of course, she trained herself. She probably always wrote. There are passages in her work describing the activities of the young writer. Orlando, for instance, " was describing, as all young poets are for ever describing, nature." In a review of Kipling's *Letters of Travel* she says, " Between the ages of sixteen and twenty-one, speaking roughly, every writer keeps a large note-book devoted entirely to landscape. Words must be found for a moonlit sky, for a stream, for plane-trees after rain. They ' must ' be found. Nothing can exist unless it is properly described." That seems like autobiography.

But, even more important, she had the free run of her father's library. It was a splendid library, catholic, discriminating, stocked with the classics and containing his almost unique private collection of eighteenth-century books. Virginia was turned loose in this. She could read what she liked, and she read enormously. If her experience of life was limited, her intellectual contacts were entirely untrammelled. No notions of Victorian nicety cramped her choice of books. This freedom must have been incalculably useful to a girl who was going to be a novelist. For the novelist may have distastes and prejudices, but he must never be shocked. He must never allow life to strike him in the face and leave him injured and insulted, blind to the force which hit him.

Now one of the most remarkable qualities of Virginia Woolf's writing is its candour. Perversion and violence, madness and abnormality, vice and cruelty do not frighten her. She was never affected by that peculiar disadvantage of the woman artist with a Victorian upbringing, which arises from ignorance, *naïveté*, curiosity and resentment, combined with a fear of some dark mystery lying just beyond the borders of legitimate knowledge. For all her delicacy, sensitiveness and restricted contact with the world, she was intellectually free, candid and unafraid.

She inherited from her father another advantage. Leslie Stephen had left Cambridge owing to his agnosticism. His daughter was brought up within no orthodox religious body. Whatever the advantages and disadvantages of such inherited orthodoxy to women at other times, to artists in the twentieth century it has almost invariably proved distressing. Virginia Stephen was never faced by that conflict of loyalties which so often attends, for intelligent youth, the relinquishment of an outgrown creed. Her mind was never torn by the horrors of apostasy. It is scarred by no old wounds left by crises of faith. It preserved instead an inviolable respect for truth, respect for reason, respect for integrity of judgment.

This quality of calm, candid observation of the complex drama of the universe was fortified by another circumstance. As a girl, she formed an early acquaintance with Greek thought and literature. Walter Pater's sister taught her the Greek alphabet. She read Plato ; she read Sophocles ; and whatever respect for truth she might have inherited from her father was strengthened a thousandfold by this acquaintance with the classics.

" It is an exhausting process, to concentrate painfully upon the exact meaning of words," she wrote in " Not Knowing Greek." " To judge what each admission involves ; to follow intently, yet critically, the dwindling and changing of opinion as it intensifies into truth. Are pleasure and good the same ? Can virtue be taught ? Is virtue knowledge ? The tired or feeble mind may easily lapse as the remorseless questioning proceeds, but no one, however weak, can fail, even if he does not learn more from Plato, to love knowledge better. For as the argument mounts from step to step, Protagoras yielding, Socrates pushing on, what matters is not so much the end we reach as our manner of reaching it. That all can feel—the indomitable honesty, the courage, the love of truth which draws Socrates and us in his wake to the summit where, if we too may stand for a moment, it is to enjoy the greatest felicity of which we are capable."

This last conviction was unusual for a woman. Girls of her generation, whatever their natural inclinations, were not commonly brought up with a great regard for truth. The double standard of morality ruling Ibsen's *Doll's House* left truth outside the necessities of a woman's world. Birth, death, sickness and the care of small children, the propitiation of a lord and master, permit little leisure for that exacting occupation—the pursuit of truth. But Virginia Stephen, rambling about her father's library, reading the classics, reading Plato, had become convinced that for one woman at least, for herself, truth was important. All through her life, she has hitherto preserved, undeterred by contemporary scepticism and distrust of the intellect, a sense of absolute reality, a light of truth shining steadily beyond the shifting individualism of personal experience, illuminating all reasonable human beings, men and women, rich and poor, alike.

I believe that this early training of Virginia Stephen in Platonic philosophy and the discipline of the classics has been of the most profound importance to her later work as an artist. M. Florio Delattre, professor at Lille University, published in 1932 a scholarly and thoughtful volume of criticism, *Le Roman psychologique de Virginia Woolf*, in which he has devoted several sections to the discussion of Mrs. Woolf's philosophical affiliations with Bergson, with Proust, and with James Joyce. M. Delattre him-

self confesses that Mrs. Woolf declares she has read
no Bergson ; but he ingeniously insists that her
sister-in-law, Mrs. Karin Stephen, Adrian Stephen's
wife, has published a book upon the French
philosopher—*The Misuse of Mind : A Study of
Bergson's Attack on Intellectualism.* So he argues
that Mrs. Woolf must be at least acquainted with
Bergson's doctrines, must sympathise with his revolt
against abstract intellectualism, and demonstrates, in
her appreciation of the qualitative aspect of time, and
in her interest in the psychological importance of
" moments of time," her fundamental Bergsonianism.

It is true that Mrs. Woolf has made, in *Jacob's
Room*, in *The Mark on the Wall*, and in *A Room
of One's Own*, certain fragmentary but irreverent
comments upon academic knowledge and intellectual specialists. " And what is knowledge ?
What are our learned men save the descendants of
witches and hermits who crouched in caves and in
woods brewing herbs, interrogating shrew-mice and
writing down the language of the stars ? And the less
we honour them as our superstitions dwindle and our
respect for beauty and health of mind increases. . . . "
It is true that she is deeply interested in the odd
behaviour of time in the individual consciousness. It
is true that her methods are sometimes similar to those
of Proust, and sometimes identical with those of
Joyce. She concerns herself in her later works with
that subconscious realm in which the law of reason
does not run. She has re-created those experiences
which lie beyond the control of the intellect. But

she does not share the Bergsonian revolt against reason. She rebukes her fellow-Georgians for their unbelief. "The most sincere of them will only tell us what it is that happens to himself. They cannot make a world, because they are not free of other human beings. They cannot tell stories, because they do not believe that stories are true. They cannot generalise. They depend on their senses and emotions, whose testimony is trustworthy, rather than on their intellects, whose message is obscure. And they have perforce to deny themselves the use of some of the most powerful and some of the most exquisite of the weapons of their craft."

Thus, though she shares the preoccupations of her Bergsonian contemporaries, she approaches them from a different standpoint. It is from her belief, engendered, probably, during those early readings of Greek, in the validity of the intellectual approach to truth, that she has embarked upon her adventures into the re-creation of subconscious experience. That, I believe, is the secret of much that has been found puzzling in her studies of psychological processes. She observes " the stream of consciousness "; but she examines it with an intellectual instrument in which she, unlike many contemporary writers, has not lost her faith.

A good Platonist, she is an aristocrat, but with a sense of communal experience and social responsibility. She cherishes, it is true, an almost romantic affection for coarse and humorous old women, " jolly old fishwives " and beggars. But she does not idealise ignorance, as some modern writers do, who appear to hold that the illiterate alone hold the secret of the good life.

The Elizabethans, she assures us in *Orlando*, did not share such superstitions. " For it has to be remembered that crime and poverty had none of the attraction for the Elizabethans that they have for us. They had none of our modern shame of book-learning ; none of our belief that to be born the son of a butcher is a blessing and to be unable to read a virtue ; no fancy that what we call ' life ' and ' reality ' are somehow connected with ignorance and brutality." So far as intelligence was concerned, so far as literature was concerned, she confessed unashamedly, in one of her articles for the *Athenæum*, " it seems curious to find . . . how little one is ashamed of being . . . an unmitigated snob." In her Introduction to *Life as We have Known it*, after praising the strength, the humour, the sculpturesque quality of working women, she adds remarkably, " But, at the same time, it is much better to be a lady ; ladies desire Mozart and Einstein—that is, they desire things that are ends, not things that are means." It is a sweeping statement. " Ladies desire Mozart." Only Leslie Stephen's daughter, one feels, could have made it. For ladies so often desire things that are not ends in themselves— Derby winners, and banks of azaleas, and strings of pearls, and the chairmanships of committees to organise charity balls, and duchesses to dinner. But the ladies whom Leslie Stephen's daughter met were sure of their tastes. A confidence of culture, not only in herself, but in her readers, impregnates her work. Once, after quoting Wordsworth and Coleridge in an article, she adds, "such lines of exhortation and command spring to the memory instantly," betraying an almost pathetic confidence in the frequency of well-stocked memories. Once, writing in an American paper, she plunged into the astounding observation, " One dare scarcely say it, but it is true. Nobody knows French but the French themselves. Every second Englishman reads French."

" Every second Englishman reads French "! One thinks of every second Englishman—in Halifax and Bristol, Great Missenden and Bethnal Green. One thinks of the proportion of the population educated at elementary schools ; how that only 15 per cent. of all English boys and girls ever have any further education after leaving school at fourteen ; and of the minority of even that 15 per cent. who can read any other language but their own. And then one returns to the sentences " Every second Englishman reads French," " Ladies desire Mozart," and remembers that, even though such statements are to be taken little more seriously than the statement that nineteen English counties could be seen from Orlando's oak-tree, yet that particular hyperbole was only possible to a woman brought up as Leslie Stephen's daughter had been brought up, among people who took culture and taste, a knowledge of classical literature, and acquaintance with music and painting and language, entirely for granted.

Such an attitude was probably inevitable for one brought up as she was in a small circle of highly cultured men and women. During her father's life-time she lived the outward life of an Edwardian young lady. She poured out tea in the drawing-room. She went through the ritual of the London season. She visited her brothers for May Week at Cambridge. The tea-parties at the Hilberys', the personality of Clara Durrant in *Jacob's Room*, the whole of *Mrs. Dalloway*, appear to be reflections from this period. She learned the delicately balanced convention of intercourse in the enclosed and artificial world of London society.

But it was a particular branch of that society. The people whom she met would not regard as unimportant the preoccupations of the artist. The stultifying atmosphere of provincial Philistinism would never smother her early aspirations. The circumstances of her youth, which limited her experience of life, probably contributed to the strength of her confidence in intellectual and aesthetic values.

The life of a daughter at home, however, came to an end. In 1904 her father died, and Virginia with her sister and two brothers set up house in Bloomsbury at 46 Gordon Square. And now her latent talent began to flower. She was, for a young woman of her time, quite extraordinarily free. She had inde-pendence. She had an income. She was living with a group of people like-minded to herself. Her sister was painting. She began to write.

She was not yet ready, she felt, to produce a novel. She had read widely. She had ideas about books. Her father and his friends had written about books and writers. It was about books and writers that she began to write. For her, criticism came before creation. She had to write herself free from the scholarly tradition before she could produce original creative work. She became one of the reviewers for *The Times Literary Supplement*, a position which she has held ever since. Though she felt little confidence in her own learning, her knowledge of literary history was unusual. She did not have to write for money. She could do as much or as little as she chose. She was free to work, to read, to travel. She went to Greece, to Lisbon, to Italy. It was almost an ideal form of life for an artist. Yet she did not publish her first novel till 1915.

She was, for one thing, still extremely delicate. The physical vitality desirable to enable any young artist to break through the network of difficulties which surround even the most favoured had never been hers. But her talent was maturing, her insight into life was deepening, and when in 1912 she married the publicist, Leonard Woolf, she did not enter that domestic nunnery which isolates so many married women as surely as though they were in a religious order. Her husband believed in her talents and shared her standard of values. Where she inclined more to literature and painting, he leant rather to politics and music ; but their tastes were complementary. He seems to have displayed none of the common desire of husbands to concentrate all his wife's energy and capacity on himself. He enriched her interests while guarding her personality.

26

If her earlier interests had been exclusively artistic, it would be no longer possible for Leonard Woolf's wife to remain indifferent to politics. Little though she might care for " means rather than ends," deeply though she might share her father's dislike of taking sides, the political world surrounded her. In 1913 she toured with her husband the North Country industrial towns and attended in Newcastle the conference of Co-operative Guildswomen. She heard much of the Socialist and Co-operative and Trades Union movements. And many of her friends were suffragettes.

This last circumstance cannot have added to her ease of mind. The early years of the twentieth century were difficult for a woman who was an artist, not merely because her opportunities were restricted, but because a new distraction had been added to the thousand and one domestic responsibilities which always had been hers. There was Mrs. Fawcett—a family friend of the Stephens ; there was Lady Constance Lytton ; there were the Pankhursts. There was the whole movement for the enfranchisement of women. And while on the one hand the suffragettes opened new opportunities and suggested new interests to a woman, at the same time they summoned her to sacrifice the preoccupations of the artist. They wanted her to join in their work of enfranchising the woman citizen. It must have been distracting. How could she dare to claim leisure and security for her little, individual vision of beauty when those other women were marching in processions, waving banners, risking their health and sanity in hunger strikes ? The memoirs of Dame Ethel Smyth, the early novels of Stella Benson, of Cicely Hamilton and of Elizabeth Robins, that agonised self-revelation of Sylvia Pankhurst in her book *The Suffrage Movement*, show what could happen to any artist who was also a woman of courage, sensitiveness and public spirit. Writers, painters, musicians and actresses were torn between their obligations to art and their obligations to society. The more sensitive and intelligent they were, the more clearly they recognised that even the further perfection of their art depended upon its proper social environment. They could not write, could not paint, could not compose symphonies, conduct great orchestras, produce great spectacles, while handicapped by those conditions against which they were summoned to do battle. Yet, while speaking and marching and organising processions and lobbying Members of Parliament, they could not possibly maintain that equilibrium and concentration which are necessary for an artist, in order that the form may burn up and make incandescent all the matter of her work, in order that she may subdue experience to comprehended beauty.

If this had been all, it would have been enough. But it was not all. An Edwardian girl might have escaped from the toils of domestic obligation and political propaganda by saying to herself, " I am a human being. I am an artist. My allegiance is to beauty, and to the discovery and creation of her diverse forms. I will write. I will paint. I will compose music. For, after all, there are many who can produce children and march in processions, but I alone have seen my own individual vision of reality and of beauty."

But a woman who was a Georgian was not to be left in peace to her claim of immunity. If the Georgians had deposed the Reason, they had discovered the Nerves. They had discovered sensibilities and intuitions, and memories, and the subconscious mind, and sex. Particularly they had discovered sex. At the very moment when an artist might have climbed out of the traditional limitations of domestic obligation by claiming to be a human being, she was thrust back into them by the authority of the psychologist. A woman, she was told, must enjoy the full cycle of sex-experience, or she would become riddled with complexes like a rotting fruit. Her impulses, her convictions, every notion that entered her head came to her, somehow or other, from her womanhood. Her sex was all that really mattered about her. Women were even called " The Sex." " The facts of life " were supposed to indicate the facts of sex. If it were true, as the suffragettes began to tell women, that men and women differed in the physical phenomenon of their sex alone, then, since this physical phenomenon was held to be by far the most important thing about them, it must be also true that their differences were much greater than their likenesses. Their common humanity shrank to a small and unreliable generalisation ; their physical differences isolated them eternally. There they stood, separated by the unbridgeable gulf of sex. They could not possibly understand each other, having no common ground of experience. Women were a "mystery" to men ; the "understanding" of men occupied a large part of the attention of women, and even so was never completely accomplished. Indeed, taking it by and large, it was marvellous that they had ever contrived to live together for so long on the same planet at all—though "living together" had come to signify only the habit of sexual intercourse.

All these things added to the predicament of the Georgian novelist who was a woman. There she stood, aware of her humanity, and seeing her humanity denied ; summoned to fight in a political battle, and assured that political battles were all futile ; urged to treat character as a novelist's first consideration, and conscious that character was daily changing ; anxious to devote herself, with whole-hearted integrity, to her art, and distracted by a thousand practical interests from that devotion. All the doubts and repudiations of those who reacted against the Edwardian tradition were hers, combined with all the tumult of the conflict surging round Mrs. Fawcett and the Pankhursts. The full weight of the Freudian revelation fell upon her head. She was told to write like a human being, to write like a woman, to write like a political propagandist, and not to write at all. The confusion and conflict were immeasurably disturbing. The wonder is that any woman continued to write novels at all.

Virginia Woolf, of course, was vividly aware of all these distractions. She was a critic. She lived in London among those people who are particularly influenced by the spirit of the age. She was herself exceedingly sensitive to changing moods and to the dictates and caprices of the time spirit. But her particular form of training and the circumstances of her life, her belief in the human communism of intellectual experience, as well as her natural inclinations, fortified her. Against the insidious suggestions of psychologists, she took her stand on her conviction of a humanity stronger in its spiritual unity than in its sexual difference. Her particular theory of the sexes, which later she was to work out in *Orlando* and *A Room of One's Own*, gave her a weapon against that adversary of creative art.

But she had to face the political demand as well. She was far too intelligent and honest to remain unaware of the importance of the Suffrage movement. Little as she liked its external manifestations, greatly though administrative activities might bore her, she was awake to their significance. At the Guildswoman Conference, she confessed in her Introduction to *Life as We have Known it* that she was irritated and depressed in the extreme by the thought that " in all that audience, among all those women who worked, who bore children, who scrubbed and cooked and bargained, there was not a single woman with a vote. Let them fire off their rifles if they liked, but they would hit no target ; there were only blank cartridges inside." She was aware of the impotence and indignity of disenfranchisement. She paid her tribute to the women fighting against it in her portrait of Mary Datchet, the suffrage worker, in *Night and Day*. She understood well the conflict between art and politics, between action for immediate relief of material

conditions, and action to create enduring beauty.
Mrs. Dalloway's description of her own confusions ;
Richard Dalloway's confession to Rachel Vinrace that
he was prouder of securing an extra hour off for factory
girls than of having " written Keats and Shakespeare
into the bargain " ; Orlando's conviction that not
eight-hour days, and covenants and Acts of Parliament,
but something wild and gay and splendid, like a bed
of hyacinths, was what people needed—all these, and
a dozen other references, bear witness to her sense of
conflict.

Yet for herself she was clear enough—clearer perhaps in intention than in action. She chose to be an
artist, to concern herself with ends and not with means.
Her personal preferences, her inherited predilections,
and her physical disabilities determined her. She
was too fragile to stand the strain of that double life
which invested William Butler Yeats with a senator's
dignity, set George Bernard Shaw to reorganise the
Fabian Society, or earlier on plunged Victor Hugo
into the whirlpool of French politics. She could do
only one thing at a time, and that with difficulty. But
her knowledge of the conflict, her continual contact
with people interested in its other side, her own sense
of reality and of the importance of human beings,
kept her feet firmly on the ground. Even when her
prose experiments were to outsoar the most daring
flights of her contemporaries, her imagination was
firmly based upon the common experiences of human
life. She knew that working women have need of
political protection, that working men enjoy a poorer

diet than that of college girls, that artists need privacy and adequate incomes, that miners' lives are complicated by coal-dust and the lack of bathing accommodation. Her contact with the political world might never deter her from her single-hearted determination to serve truth and beauty ; but it undoubtedly enriched and amplified that service. The temptation to be precious, the temptation to be rarefied, and abstract and detached from life, had far less power over her because one side of her mind was continually rubbing up against the minds of people engaged in securing pit-head baths for miners, educational scholarships for women, or a higher standard of administration in the colonies.

She was brought into direct contact with many of these interests through the Hogarth Press, which she and her husband founded for the printing and publication of books. At first it was installed at Hogarth House in Richmond where they lived during the war, and there she helped to produce work by Katherine Mansfield, John Middleton Murry, T. S. Eliot and E. M. Forster, as well as her own essays, sometimes with decorations by her sister. But later, when the press had been moved to London, it issued also political criticism of a radical character, her husband's studies, Norman Leys' *Kenya*, Lord Olivier's studies of Imperialism, and a formidable list of highly controversial books.

This indirect connection with the world of action must have been immensely beneficial to her work as a novelist ; for she had to live a very quiet life, with-

33   C

drawn from commonplace activities. She suffered, while at Richmond, from periods of illness during which she was able to do very little writing, sometimes none at all. The war passed over her. In 1915 she published her first novel, in 1919 her second. They did not attract wide attention. She began working at essays and sketches in a new style. In 1919 she published *The Mark on the Wall* and *Kew Gardens*. Two years after she collected these, with other experimental pieces, in the volume called *Monday or Tuesday*. The following year she produced *Jacob's Room*.

That established her reputation. Previously she had been known to a small circle of friends. Now the whole intelligent English-reading public began to discuss her work. Since then each new publication has increased her prestige. To-day few men and no women hold a comparable position in contemporary English letters. She has published four other novels : *Mrs. Dalloway*, *To the Lighthouse*, *Orlando*, and *The Waves* ; in 1929 the essay *A Room of One's Own* ; in 1932 the *Letter to a Young Poet*. She has collected a volume of critical essays, and written various articles and short sketches for *The Athenæum*, *The Nation*, the American *New Republic*, *The London Mercury*, *Time and Tide*, *The New Statesman*, the New York *Dial*, and still continues her scholarly essays for *The Times Literary Supplement*. She has written introductions for republished classics, such as Sterne's *Sentimental Journey*, or for new work which needed some special explanation. With the help of S. S. Koteliansky she has prepared English versions of

Goldenveizer's *Talks with Tolstoi,* a collection of Tolstoi's own *Love - Letters,* and Dostoevsky's *Stavrogin's Confession.* She acts as fiction reader for the Hogarth Press. She has read papers on literary subjects in London and Cambridge. She has very occasionally spoken at public meetings.

After the war she and her husband moved from Richmond to Bloomsbury and brought the Hogarth Press with them. It continues to form one of their main interests. Its equipment occupies a large part of the tall house in which they live, raised above the neighbouring square as it were, on a mountain of literature. Mrs. Woolf herself uses as a study an immense half-subterranean room behind the house, piled with books, parcels, packets of unbound volumes, and manuscripts from the press. There too are stored great canvases by her sister or other artists, which no smaller apartment could contain. There one seems to move among books and papers as among the rocks and ledges of that submarine cave of which the characters in her books are always dreaming. The light penetrates wanly down between the high buildings overhead, as through deep waters, and noises from the outside world enter only in a subdued murmur, as from very far away.

She lives quietly. Her public appearances are rare, but they are notably successful ; and her remoteness only enhances her prestige. Tall, graceful, exceedingly slender, she creates an impression of curbed but indestructible vitality. An artist, sitting near her during a series of concerts given by the Léner quartette, said afterwards, " She makes me think of a frozen falcon ; she is so still, and so alert." The description does in some measure suggest her elegance veiling such intellectual decision, her shyness lit by such irony. Meeting all contacts with the world lightly yet courageously ; withdrawn, but not disdainful ; in love with experience yet exceedingly fastidious ; detached, yet keenly, almost passionately interested ; she watches the strange postures and pretences of humanity, preserving beneath her formidable dignity and restraint a generosity, a belief, and a radiant acceptance of life unsurpassed by any living writer.

II
THE UNCOMMON READER

VIRGINIA STEPHEN began her career as a reviewer for *The Times Literary Supplement*. It is as a critic that many still prefer to regard Virginia Woolf. Certainly she has written as much criticism as fiction, and her novels and sketches contribute to her critical theories ; for with her, theory and practice have walked hand in hand. What she has urged upon others, she has attempted herself, and what she has herself attempted, she has noted, watched, and appraised in others.

The functions of a critic and his methods are a matter of ancient controversy. Mrs. Woolf herself forestalled any too grandiloquent claim by calling her first collection of critical essays *The Common Reader*, and professing this modest estimate of her qualities. " The Common Reader," she said, borrowing the title from Dr. Johnson, " differs from the critic and the scholar. He is worse educated, and nature has not gifted him so generously. He reads for his own pleasure rather than to impart knowledge or correct the opinion of others. Above all, he is guided by an instinct to create for himself, out of whatever odds or ends he can come by, some kind of a whole—a portrait of a man, a sketch of an age, a theory of the art of writing." And this has ever been her own way with books.

It is true that hitherto she has formulated no

critical system. She has produced no confession, foreshadowing future developments, comparable to T. S. Eliot's *For Lancelot Andrewes*. She associates herself with no orthodox school of thought. Many of her essays and reviews have a light, casual air, and when collected and compared, they abound in trivial contradictions. In *The Mark on the Wall*, for instance, she condemns generalisations, likening them to those Sunday walks, Sunday luncheons and " the habit of sitting all together in one room until a certain hour, although nobody liked it," familiar to every English family. Yet in *The Common Reader* she reproves the present age for its inability to generalise, explaining that because of this the Georgians are imprisoned in their own personalities, instead of being free of humanity. She condemns, in her essay on *Robinson Crusoe*, the biographical method of criticism ; yet she herself dearly delights in showing how Thomas Browne kept maggots in boxes and collected coins ; how the Duchess of Newcastle wore her clothes, or how George Eliot's flight with Lewes affected her novels. She praises the intellect, yet thinks little of learning. Sometimes one would detect Sainte Beuve with his system of biographical interpretation as her master ; sometimes Aristotle and his classical disciples, with their metaphysical codes.

Her preferences are dictated by no detectable fashion. She chooses where she will. If she praises Donne, she will not dispraise Shelley. She acknowledges the greatness of the early nineteenth century.

Her love for the Elizabethans has not blinded her to the excellence of Swift or Montaigne, Flaubert or Defoe. Chaucer and Jane Austen, Tolstoi and Sterne, Shakespeare and Sophocles—she hails them all. Her admirations move where her spirit blows them, fastidious, eclectic and individual.

Yet she is a fine critic ; perhaps even a great one. Her influence over contemporary letters is as strong as that of any writer of her generation, and it is a vital influence, making for adventurousness, humanity and reason. No attentive reader of her essays could fail to derive from them a deeper respect for truth, a higher sensitiveness to beauty, and an enlarged understanding of the art of literature.

The qualities which underlie her influence are rare ones—though less rare separately than in their combination.

She is, of course, exceedingly well informed. She has achieved that " acquaintance with the best possible " which Matthew Arnold prescribed as the proper diet for critics, by reading widely, reading intensively and reading little but the best of English, French and Greek literatures, from an early age ; she has studied the Russian masters in translation ; she has lived among people before whom the whole range of European literature is spread like a familiar map, so that at any moment they can point, even if blindfolded, to this hill, that valley, that turn of the road ; and she can herself join in the sport.

Her scholarship has been well assimilated. She wears it lightly. Taught by her mistrust of the

39

twisted old men of Cambridge, whom she has exposed in *Jacob's Room* and *A Society*, she looks upon academic learning with suspicion. But at the same time a personal diffidence makes her regard herself as insecurely educated. Almost too sensitive to her own limited experience, she feels ignorant of life, forced to distil truth very carefully, hoarding its precious drops, gathered from the few herbs and bones and minerals which she has collected with difficulty but with joy. No critic who felt like that about herself could be didactic. She could never become shrill, like Matthew Arnold, nor transcendental like Coleridge, nor pontifical like Johnson. But if she lacks their priestly authority, she gains an intimacy and humanity which were never theirs.

She has, moreover, an almost perfect taste. Few critics have ever been more alert to detect humbug, the spurious, the second rate ; few have been more generously and freshly appreciative of real merit, even if it appears under strange disguises. Taste for her is a natural gift, never blunted by the adolescent ignorance, the commercial pressure, the confusion of aim and distractions of fashion, to which so many critical judgments are subjected. She has been all her life above the journalistic battle ; it has been unnecessary for her to flatter cliques or propitiate advertisers, to compromise with moralists or defend causes. The detachment which Matthew Arnold demanded for the critic, but of which he himself was temperamentally incapable, has always been hers. And it has been guided by that unerring eye which is as much a gift of nature as a perfect sense of musical pitch, or an infallible judgment of the direction of a tennis ball.

But though her touch is light, her intention is profoundly serious. She has discarded the pontifical robes and manner because she is modest, and because she has a sense of humour ; not because her sense of solemnity is lacking. There was more than fantasy in her picture of Orlando in the chapel, recalling how a writer has his own religion and his own code of morals, in which the excessive addiction to the too frequent use of the letter S or the present participle may be major sins. Reviewing the letters of the twentieth-century Sir Walter Raleigh, she shows fine scorn for his lack of real interest in literature. She has little use for a professor of literature who was so much interested in life that he had no time for art. The creation of good people and of good books, as she says in *A Society*, are the two most important human purposes ; and they are not easily separable. For art, to her, is an extension of reality. The artist prays " once in a way to wrap up in a book something so hard, so rare, one could swear it was life's meaning." His concern is with the soul ; his first essential virtue is integrity.

As for what reality is, she shows herself less confident. The waiting sentinel in her mind, always ready to challenge unjustified generalisations, has made her qualify her definitions.

" What is meant by ' reality ' ? " she asks at the end of *A Room of One's Own*. " It would seem to be something very erratic, very undependable—now to be found in a dusty road, now in a scrap of newspaper in the street, now a daffodil in the sun . . . But whatever it touches, it fixes and makes permanent. That is what remains over when the skin of the day has been cast into the hedge ; that is what is left of the past time and of our loves and hates. Now the writer, as I think, has the chance to live more than other people in the presence of this reality. It is his business to find it and collect it and communicate it to the rest of us. So at least I infer from reading *Lear* or *Emma* or *La Recherche du Temps Perdu.*"

This extension of reality is a solemn business, and art, which enables man to do it, is a religious exercise, to be performed with all the force and intensity of which he is capable. She is inexorable in her demand for sincerity. Devotion to the idea must be absolute. When she condemns the modern essayist, it is for his lack of devotion to an idea. When she criticises the novels written by most women at the beginning of the nineteenth century, it is because they wrote with " a mind which was slightly pulled from the straight and made to alter its clear vision in deference to external authority." Such deference is fatal ; such divided purpose, treachery. For the artist is concerned with an individual vision of the truth which it is his obligation to reveal and make permanent and communicate to the rest of us. To concern himself rather with competition or popularity, or the approval of some extraneous authority, is the mark of an immature " private school " mind, where the pupils take sides and run only for a cup. To the mature artist she says : " to sacrifice a hair of the head of your vision, a shade of its colour, in deference to some headmaster with a silver pot in his hand or to some professor with a measuring rod up his sleeve, is the most abject treachery, and the sacrifice of wealth and chastity, which used to be said to be the greatest of human disasters, a mere flea-bite in comparison."

This is strong language, but she feels strongly. That devotion to integrity which she early learned from Plato dictates her artistic as well as her intellectual standard of values. She sees truth as an organic as well as a revealing thing, a light which is also life, the quenching of which means death. In her own picture of her mind at work in *Monday or Tuesday*, she shows herself " desiring truth, awaiting it, laboriously distilling a few words, for ever desiring . . ." Disloyalty to truth is, then, the cardinal sin.

But the artist is concerned also with beauty. Form is important. A statute of parliament may be true, but it is not beautiful. Its form is utilitarian ; it is not aesthetic. Mrs. Woolf's own long and exciting quest for ever new forms of prose-expression has been conducted simultaneously with her pursuit, as a critic, of the secret of form. And one thing it has taught her. If the first essential of good art is truth, the second is that the form must burn up the idea. The novelist, she said, reviewing a novel by G. B. Stern, " is terribly exposed to life. . . . Stridently, clamorously, life is for ever pleading that she is the proper end of fiction and that the more he sees of her, and catches of her,

43

the better his book will be. She does not add, however, that she is grossly impure," and Mrs. Woolf
shows how, unless we can resolve the fleeting moment
into something stable and enduring, it escapes us, as
foxtrots and last year's fashions have escaped. Whatever facts, emotions and experiences the artist tastes,
he must digest completely. The mind must be master
of its material. " There must be no obstacle in it,
no foreign matter unconsumed. . . . The reason why
we know so little of Shakespeare . . . is that his
grudges and spites and antipathies are hidden from us.
We are not held up by some ' revelation ' which reminds us of the writer. All desire to protest, to
preach, to proclaim an injury, to pay off a score, to
make the world a witness of some hardship or grievance
was fired out of him and consumed. Therefore his
poetry flows from him free and unimpeded. If ever
a human being got his work expressed completely, it
was Shakespeare. If ever a mind was incandescent,
unimpeded . . . it was Shakespeare's mind." This
is her test of disinterestedness. There must be no
anger in a work of art, and no aggression. It must be
an end in itself, as perfect and self-contained as a Greek
vase. One of her complaints against the Edwardians
was that their novels were not ends in themselves.
" In order to complete them it seems necessary to do
something—to join a Society, or, more desperately, to
write a cheque. . . . But with the work of other
novelists it is different. *Tristram Shandy* or *Pride and
Prejudice* is complete in itself ; it is self-contained ; it
leaves one with no desire to do anything except indeed

to read the book again, and to understand it better. The difference perhaps is that both Sterne and Jane Austen were interested in things in themselves ; in character itself ; in the book in itself ; . . . But the Edwardians were never interested in character itself, or in the book in itself. They were interested in something outside."

Now here she is perhaps upon less certain ground. In asking that a work of art should be " an end in itself," she is not so much asking for something that is undesirable as for something that is impossible. Disgusted by art which is insincere, which is tendencious, which is " pulled from the straight by deference to external authority," she condemns John Galsworthy, H. G. Wells and Arnold Bennett because their works induced their readers to sign cheques and join societies.

It is true that she has strong support for her demand. That art should be an " end in itself " was the cry of Arnold, of Pater, of the French Symbolists, and of almost all her own contemporaries, the Georgian critics. The business of the artist, says one of them, R. A. Scott James, putting the theory into a nutshell, " is to provide us with an experience, and . . . any end he may have beyond making that experience vivid and complete is an alien end, destroying his singleness of purpose, wholly disruptive of his art and destructive of his energy."

But directly we say that the business of the artist is to provide us with a vivid and complete experience, no more, no less, we reopen the whole question.

45

What sort of experience, we may ask, and how is he to make it vivid and complete ? Behind the choice of what experience he shall offer us lie other choices, between one sense and another, between the senses and the reason, between optimism and pessimism, between black and white. Morality lies behind it, and an ethical as well as an aesthetic convention. Further, beyond such a choice lies the influence that it must have upon its readers. The morality of the artist which affected his choice may differ from the morality of his work, which affects his readers. But both must be considered ; and Mrs. Woolf herself has been driven, by her own sense of truth and reality, to recognise this. She lay down a sharp line of distinction between the Edwardians and Sterne or Jane Austen in one essay ; but directly she began to deal with the facts instead of the theory her sharp line quivered. For one thing, she could not disguise even from herself the fact that though art may be, theoretically, an "end in itself," it concerns morality. Writing another essay, on *Chaucer and the Pastons*, she has said, " For among writers there are two kinds : there are the priests who lead you straight up to the mystery : there are the laymen who imbed their doctrines in flesh and blood and make a complete model of the world without excluding the bad or laying stress upon the good. Wordsworth, Coleridge and Shelley are among the priests. . . . But Chaucer lets us go our way doing the ordinary things with ordinary people. His morality lies in the way men and women behave to each other. We see them eating, drinking, laughing and making love, and come to feel without a word being said what their standards are and so are steeped through and through with their morality. There can be no more forcible preaching than this. . . . It is the morality of ordinary intercourse, the morality of the novel, which parents and librarians rightly judge to be far more persuasive than the morality of poetry." The morality of novels . . . the morality of poetry. We cannot escape them. We may cling to a doctrine of pure aesthetics as closely as we choose, but the thing is round us ; the watchdogs of the Lord bark at our heels ; the yoke of His burden is laid upon our shoulders. And Mrs. Woolf knows it. She knows that there is, at bottom, no division. In her lovely and most discerning valediction to Joseph Conrad she writes of how his critics complained that he was self-conscious and stiff, and that " the sound of his own voice was dearer to him than the voice of humanity in its anguish." She answers, " that beauty teaches, that beauty is a disciplinarian, how are we to convince them, since her teaching is inseparable from the sound of her voice and to that they are deaf ? But read Conrad . . . and he must be lost indeed to the meaning of words who does not hear in that rather stiff and sombre music, with its reserve, its pride, its vast and implacable integrity, how it is better to be good than bad, how loyalty is good and honesty and courage, though ostensibly Conrad is concerned merely to show us the beauty of a night at sea."

" Ostensibly." Is that all the difference ? For good

or evil, with or against our wills, we all are moralists, poets and novelists, Christians and Satanists, Stoics and Epicureans, Baudelaire and Dante, Sophocles and Chaucer, Jane Austen and Marcel Proust. Some proclaim the moral, Wordsworth and Coleridge, Dickens and Tolstoi. Others let it take possession of the reader's imagination unawares. But the moral is there and will have its effect. Tragedy will purify or debase the passions, as the Greeks told us ; beauty is a disciplinarian ; comedy quickens intelligence and civilises perception.

As for Sterne, with all his interest in " the book in itself ; in character itself," he based *A Sentimental Journey* on " something fundamentally philosophic." Mrs. Woolf said as much in an introduction she wrote for that work in 1928—four years after she published *Mr. Bennett and Mrs. Brown.* " It is true that it was a philosophy that was much out of fashion in the Victorian age—the philosophy of pleasure. . . . The wretch had the audacity to cry through the mouth of one of his characters, ' Mais vive la joie . . . Vive l'amour, et vive la bagatelle.' " As for Jane Austen, her sense of ethical values was so exquisitely adjusted, so sound, so strong, that she inevitably imposes it upon her readers. She imposed it upon Mrs. Woolf, who must return to it again and again in her criticism ; who uses as a torch to illumine her own standard of behaviour a scene from *The Watsons.* " But of what is it all composed ? Of a ball in a country town ; a few couples meeting and taking hands in an assembly room ; a little eating and drinking ; and for catastrophe, a boy being snubbed by one young lady and kindly treated by another. . . ." " There comes a moment—' I will dance with you,' says Emma—which rises higher than the rest, which, though not eloquent in itself, or violent, or made striking by beauty of language, has the whole weight of the book behind it." " Only believe . . . that a nice girl will instinctively try to soothe the feelings of a boy who has been snubbed at a dance, and then, if you believe it implicitly and unquestioningly, you will not only make people a hundred years later feel the same thing, but you will make them feel it as literature. For certainty of that kind is the condition which makes it possible to write. To believe that your impressions hold good for others is to be released from the cramp and confinement of personality." Those three quotations are gathered from three different essays written at three different times—on *Jane Austen*, *On Not Knowing Greek*, on *How it Strikes a Contemporary*. They provide unmistakeable evidence of the ethical impression left by Jane Austen's mind on Mrs. Woolf's. They show that to her at least such an impression was important.

A work of art is not destroyed because its secondary influence upon those who encounter it is moral and persuasive. Galsworthy's play *Justice* does not fail because it has driven stall-holders to sign cheques for the Howard League of Penal Reform ; if it has weaknesses they lie elsewhere, in its sentiment or its construction or in the lack of vitality in its characterisation. The effect of a patient and intelligent reading of

Persuasion may well be to send a modern young woman to join the " Equal Rights International " ; and certainly the *Divina Comedia* has drawn young men into the bosom of the Catholic Church. Indeed, it was Dante's hope for the poem that it might do so ; just as it was Milton's hope that his *Paradise Lost* might save endangered souls.

Therefore, if we are to seek the faults of the Edwardian novelists we must find them in something more than their tendency to make their readers wish to complete them by writing cheques or joining societies. We may say that their form is clumsy, their aim confused and their morality ignoble—though the proof might be a little difficult. Mrs. Woolf, however, in an essay on *Modern Fiction* did herself find a more satisfactory definition of their failure. Taking, as usual, Wells, Bennett and Galsworthy for her victims, she decides that " if we tried to formulate our meaning in one word we should say that these three writers are materialists. It is because they are concerned not with the spirit but with the body that they have disappointed us, and left us with the feeling that the sooner English fiction turns its back on them, as politely as may be, and marches, if only into the desert, the better for its soul." They write, she decides, of unimportant things. The destiny of Arnold Bennett's Clayhangers and Cannons is " an eternity of bliss spent in the very best hotel in Brighton " ; of H. G. Wells she asks, " What more damaging criticism can there be both of his earth and of his Heaven than that they are to be inhabited here and hereafter by his

Joans and his Peters ? " She accuses them of coarseness of perception and indifference to the affairs of the spirit.

She may not be just in her estimate of individual novels here. I hardly think she is. But in her opposition to materialism she is on far surer ground ; yet she has made her former position untenable. The aesthetic method differs from the didactic, but both are subject to ethical judgment. Beauty of the spirit, " soul " as she defines it in her essay on *The Russian Point of View*, character, as she repeats continually, is the final test. But for the conditions which make beauty and integrity possible, she is driven back to consider matters which are means to ends, and not ends in themselves. *A Room of One's Own* at once contradicts and confirms her criticism. Seeing that to produce good work, freedom of mind, independence, privacy and leisure, a training for truth instead of for docility, all are necessary, she herself returns to discuss the contingent, the ephemeral. For the truth, of course, is that during our mortal life, while souls still rest in bodies, absolute and contingent are bound up together. We can live neither on bread alone, nor without bread. We cannot see truth when frightened of starvation. We cannot extend our vision of reality without a room of our own. We hunger for the absolute. Saint Augustine's cry still holds us, " Thou madest us for Thyself and we have no rest until we rest in Thee " : but we are bound in mortality, prisoners in a world of compromise, where politics and aesthetics meet, where mercy and truth must kiss each

other. Life, and the means of life ; beauty and sani-
tation ; integrity of vision and sickness-insurance ;
the abstract metaphysics of criticism and the financial
difficulties of higher education for women, are all
bound up together. It is to Mrs. Woolf's honour as
a critic that she has seen it so, and that, in spite of her
natural predilection for the absolute, the abstract and
the spiritual, she should, in *A Room of One's Own* and
her introduction to *Life as We have Known It*, have
recognised the humble foundations from which great
literatures rise.

For if such are the general principles upon which
Mrs. Woolf bases her judgment of literature, she holds
certain theories about her contemporaries which have
had, and are having, considerable influence on their
development. It is true that she sees each artist's
vision of reality as individual. " All alone we must
climb upon the novelist's shoulders and gaze into his
eyes," she says, in that essay on *Robinson Crusoe* which
also contains her indictment of the biographical
method, " until we, too, understand in what order he
ranges the large common objects upon which novelists
are fated to gaze—man and men, nature, and, behind
or above, the power which is conveniently called God."
She bids us observe how writers living at the same time
—say Scott, Jane Austen and Peacock—order the
differing perspectives of their universe.

Reality is to be found ; reality is individual ; but
not for a moment will she let us forget that the individual stands in time. His roots are in tradition.
Though Peacock and Scott may bring forth different

fruit, they are both rooted in the same soil. Had the age been different, their work would have been changed.

She is, as it happens, enormously aware of time. Throughout her novels time clangs like fate ; its sound reverberates with terrifying persistence. When Jacob, when Mrs. Dalloway, when Orlando hear clocks strike, the explosion shakes the complex fabric of their being. The whole of *Orlando* is a fantasia on the time sense.

Nobody so sensitive to the striking of clocks could remain indifferent to the influence of tradition. She is vividly conscious of the characteristics of the Georgian age as she sees it.

She has been accused of making too narrow a survey of that age. Her eyes are fixed, some say, on a little clique of intellectuals, the whole sum of whose work is hardly discernible by the general public. Her justification is, probably, that she is dealing with a tendency rather than with a generation. In speaking of Georgian literature she is regarding only those writers who have reacted against the literary doctrines which were orthodox before the war—before 1910, she would say. She is looking at the writers who have definitely repudiated something bequeathed them by the past generation, and added to their inheritance something new.

The Georgians, she said in *Mr. Bennett and Mrs. Brown*, have to break something down before they can build their own palaces. Everywhere she hears the sound of that destruction. " Grammar is violated ;

syntax disintegrated ; as a boy staying with an aunt for the week-end rolls in the geranium bed out of sheer desperation as the solemnities of the Sabbath wear on." Hence the indecencies of James Joyce, the obscurity of T. S. Eliot and, in Lytton Strachey, the " effort and strain of writing against the grain and current of the time."

What they are breaking is the tradition of description, of extraneous interests and of materialism handed down by the Edwardians. It is significant that she always confines her Edwardians to Wells, Bennett and Galsworthy. She hardly mentions Shaw, except to say that his new attitude to social values was a sign of the general disintegration which makes things hard for Georgians. I have found no trace of her estimate of George Moore.

Her contemporaries, D. H. Lawrence, T. S. Eliot, E. M. Forster, Lytton Strachey and the rest of them, she considered to be engaged in a work of destruction and suffering the usual inconveniences of that task. "Nothing happens to us as it did to our ancestors ; events are seldom important ; if we recount them, we do not really believe in them." So the Georgians have lost the art of story-telling. Only David Garnett she finds " a natural story-teller " as opposed to " self-conscious " story-tellers like Masefield.

As for the essayists, they suffer from lack of fierce attachment to anything in itself. " They share the contemporary dilemma—that lack of an obstinate conviction which lifts ephemeral sounds through the misty sphere of anybody's language to the land where

there is a perpetual marriage, a perpetual union."
And in the article where she says this, she flays alive
Hilaire Belloc, E. V. Lucas and J. C. Squire so gently
that they might never know that their flesh had been
left bare.

Georgians cannot tell stories, cannot write essays;
they are not free of each other's consciousness; they
dare not generalise; they cannot create character.
Though they distrust their intellects and trust only
their senses, it is their very senses that they have
starved. Their eyes are half-blind; their ears half-
deaf. Words, sights, sounds, scents no longer make
on them that stinging impact which led to the word-
coining genius of the Elizabethans, who wrote " as if
thought plunged into a sea of words and came up
dripping." In short, the Georgians, she is clear, are
in a bad way.

It is true that she is surrounded by sounds of
wailing and prophets of disaster. The present
fashion is not to expect masterpieces. The typical
Georgian is disgusted by his contemporary world.
He is disgusted by a " machine age," by democracy,
by urban civilisation, by the cinematograph, by
advertisement campaigns and the broadening interests
of women. D. H. Lawrence poured the dark waters
of his disgust upon us; Aldous Huxley mocks us
with more fastidious disdain; T. S. Eliot's nightingale sings " Jug, Jug " to dirty ears.

But Mrs. Woolf is no pessimist. In her *Letter
to a Young Poet* she advises her friend John, " never
think yourself singular, never think your own case

55

much harder than other people's." She refuses to accept his supposed protest that " it has never been so hard to write poetry as it is to-day." On the contrary, she envies him his opportunity, tells him that old gentlemen who say that art is dead choke themselves on their own buttered toast, and waves him on to further conquests.

That is her great virtue. That is her claim to leadership. For though satire and mockery have their value, expectation is a nobler attitude than disgust, and provides a livelier impetus to creation. In an imperfect world, it takes clearer sight and longer vision to see, beyond the limitations of the human spirit, its possibilities. It requires greater courage, magnanimity and discipline for an intelligent mind to hail the future than to despair of this present age.

But Mrs. Woolf sees cause for hope where others see only food for despair. In the first place she is herself an experimentalist and welcomes all experiment. As a critic, she will not reprove George Meredith for his lyricism nor Sterne for his irrelevance. She is a prose writer. She prefers to deal with modern prose rather than with verse. Yet she anticipates new forms of prose ever more closely allied to poetry. With keen adventurousness she hails even crude attempts to achieve new forms of beauty. All the excitement, disintegration, innovation and novelty of the present age urge her to hope.

She shares in and sympathises with another aspect of her period—the new contribution which women are beginning, she thinks, to make to literature. She

has none of the disbelief shown by Mrs. Humphry
Ward or Gertrude Bell in the general aptitude of
women. She welcomes with joyful enthusiasm their
growing independence, their new opportunities, and
in *A Room of One's Own* not only confesses her
faith in their future but contributes to its possibility.

She welcomes another coming change—the advent
into literature of a working-class become articulate.
Her attitude here is rather complicated ; and, indeed,
the situation confronting her is not simple. Temperamentally she is an aristocrat. She is highly sensitive
to social distinctions, to heredity, to noble blood, and
the prestige of royalty. The delicate gradations
separating the Hilberys from the Denhams, the
Ramsays from Charles Tansley, occupy perhaps an
undue place in her novels. She believes that " it is
better to be a lady," yet her whole influence as a
critic has been used to widen, not to narrow, the circle
of artists. She welcomes newcomers. She desires
change.

She looks upon contemporary England, and sees
how, if the poor to-day are shut out, the well-to-do
are shut in. " Because our baker calls and we pay
our bills with cheques and our clothes are washed for
us, and we do not know the liver from the lights, we
are condemned to remain for ever shut up in the confines of the middle classes, wearing tail coats and silk
stockings, and called Sir or Madam as the case may
be, when we are all, in truth, simply Johns and Susans.
And they remain equally deprived. For we have
as much to give them as they to give us—wit and

57

detachment, learning and poetry, and all those good gifts which those who have never answered bells or minded machines enjoy by right. But the barrier is impassable. And nothing perhaps exacerbated us more at the Congress " (it was the Guildswomen's Congress of 1913) " than the thought that this force of theirs, this smouldering heat which broke the crust now and then, and licked the surface with a hot and fearless flame, is about to break through and melt us together so that life will be richer and books more complex and society will pool its possessions instead of segregating them—all this is going to happen inevitably . . . but only when we are dead."

Her vision of segregation is excessive. Her estimate of the ladies' gift to society is flattering. The " breaking through " process, accelerated by the war, is taking place far more rapidly than Mrs. Woolf anticipated. The letter from which this passage was taken was written in 1930, when already it had become no longer necessary for those who wished otherwise to remain shut in behind the barrier of the middle classes. It is no longer " certain that, by some fault of our commonwealth, the poor poet has not in these days, nor has had for two hundred years, a dog's chance." William H. Davies, Sean O'Casey, Lionel Britton, James Hanley, and to say nothing of Dickens and his bottle-factory, all belie her. But on this point, perhaps, she could counter our objection with the theory of William Blake, often, like all the greatest mystics, capable of the most practical common sense. Writing an introduction to a catalogue of pictures, he remarked, " Some people and not a few artists have asserted that the Painter of this Picture would not have done so well if he had been properly encouraged. Let those who think so reflect on the State of Nations under Poverty and their incapability of Art ; tho' Art is above either, the Argument is better for Affluence than Poverty : and tho' he could not have been a greater artist, yet he could have produced greater works of Art in proportion to his means."

In short, she welcomes the pooling of experience, she welcomes the breaking down of barriers, she welcomes innovations in technique and innovations in social custom. She does not regard our present disabilities as permanent, and her optimism is founded on no superficial tolerance, but on a sober and reasoned theory of art. For she has repudiated the more brittle individualism of her contemporaries. Literature, she believes, is corporate ; its creators are not engaged merely in amusing themselves nor in finding an outlet for their repressed emotions ; they are taking part in a common task to which both writers and readers may contribute something. The real life, she says in *A Room of One's Own*, is the common life, not the little separate lives which we all live as individuals. In this real life one age ministers to another. The writers of one period prepare notebooks to be used for the finished masterpieces of another. So, in the final essay of *The Common Reader*, she gives advice to critics which transcends all smaller, casual and more petulant opinions which she may have expressed elsewhere. " Let them take

a wider, a less personal view of modern literature,"
she commands, " and look indeed upon the writers as
if they were engaged upon some vast building, which
being built by common effort, the separate workmen
may well remain anonymous. Let them slam the
door upon the cosy company where sugar is cheap
and butter plentiful, give over, for a time at least, the
discussion of that fascinating topic—whether Byron
married his sister—and, withdrawing, perhaps, a
handsbreadth from the table where we sit chattering,
say something interesting about literature itself. Let
us buttonhole them as they leave, and recall to their
memory that gaunt aristocrat, Lady Hester Stanhope,
who kept a milk-white horse in her stable in readiness
for the Messiah and was forever scanning the mountain
tops, impatiently but with confidence, for signs of his
approach, and ask them to follow her example ; scan
the horizon ; see the past in relation to the future ;
and so prepare the way for masterpieces to come."

III
" THE VOYAGE OUT "

MRS. WOOLF called her first novel *The Voyage Out*. The title, with its suggestion of movement and adventure, is significant. When so deliberate a writer indicates action, she means action. The novel is about adventure.

Its theme, indeed, is one popular among contemporary novelists. It concerns the preparation of a naïve young girl for maturity. But Mrs. Woolf's story differs in many ways from the many hundreds published each year upon this subject. It is not, so far as external circumstances are concerned, autobiographical ; it is not a liberation of repressed personal grievances against society ; and the preparation which it describes preludes not only life but death.

This is, to some extent, the theme of all her novels, except *Night and Day* and *Orlando*. In *Jacob's Room*, in *Mrs. Dalloway*, in *To the Lighthouse* and *The Waves*, she sets life against death as though thus to discern more clearly what it means. What is it that society loses when a young girl is brought through immaturity and educated as a bride, for death ? What is it that young men lose when war cuts off their life in its full blossom ? What is it that a woman experiences as she turns away from her youth towards middle age and its inevitable end ? What is it that friends lose when someone beloved by them dies ? Mrs. Woolf's five novels are written as though in answer to these questions. And the first tells the story of the young girl.

The Voyage Out has a plot. Mrs. Woolf does not really like plots. In an essay on the Elizabethan play she confesses that she finds its plot detestable, the worst effect of the influence of an Elizabethan audience on the drama. After *Night and Day* she begins to cut it out. But *The Voyage Out* is still modelled on traditional forms and tells a story of external action.

Ridley and Helen Ambrose, a classical scholar and his lovely, imperious wife, leave their children and go to spend a winter at Santa Marina on the South American coast in order that Mr. Ambrose may work quietly at his edition of *Pindar*. They travel on the ship "Euphrosene" belonging to Mr. Vinrace, Helen's brother-in-law, and with them are Vinrace himself, his daughter Rachel, a dried-up little bachelor, Mr. Pepper, and, for a short time, Clarissa and Richard Dalloway, who reappear in the later novel. Rachel is naïve and ignorant, "an unlicked girl," brought up by aunts in Richmond, musical, crude, unformed; and Helen Ambrose, intelligent and impatient, finds her rawness alarming. A brief encounter with the sentimental Dalloway shocks Rachel profoundly, and determines Helen to undertake her education. On landing at Santa Marina she carries her off to the villa on the hill, where Mr. Ambrose is to live retired, introduces her to a miscellaneous collection of English people staying at the hotel in the town, accompanies her to parties, picnics, and a trip up the river to an

Indian village, consents to her engagement to Terence
Hewet, a young English visitor at the hotel, and nurses
her through her final fatal illness. Rachel, just at the
moment when about to become a civilised woman
instead of a green girl, catches a local fever and dies.
But before the novel closes we know that though
Terence is distracted, time will comfort him ; that
Helen's heart has never really left her children ; that
St. John Hirst finds peace even in this sad enlarge-
ment of experience ; the hotel visitors look up in
sympathy from their preoccupations, and settle down
again. Life flows on over death as water closes over
a stone dropped into a pool.

It is a quiet plot. There is no conflict, no drama of
situation. The storms subside without peril to human
life ; boats arrive punctually ; meals are regular ; the
decencies of social intercourse are observed. Nobody
behaves very badly ; malice and jealousy, the extreme
limits of human passion, are not exposed. The course
of true love for the two engaged couples runs smoothly
enough. Neither misunderstanding, antagonism nor
coincidence impel the action. The sole malignancy
is that of death, and even death has dignity. It comes
as an interruption, an irrelevance ; but the interruption
is set against the even flow of events, until we see it as
part of the pattern, as a completion as well as a
catastrophe.

In *Mr. Bennett and Mrs. Brown* Mrs. Woolf declared
that the first concern of the novelist is for Character.
In *An Unwritten Novel* she showed herself led on to
the story by watching the wretched woman called

Minnie Marsh " looking at life " in a railway carriage. If we are to judge her by her own precepts, the business of *The Voyage Out* should be with character, with human beings. But character can, after all, be considered by the novelist in several quite different ways. There is the business which we call creation of character, or rather of characters, rounded, complete, flesh-and-blood human beings whose voices we hear, whose gestures we watch, whose sentiments we recognise. Becky Sharp is such a character ; Elizabeth Bennett, Madame Bovary, Anna Karenina and Maggie Tulliver are such characters. We can follow them into a life which has never been recorded ; we can imagine what they do, feel, see and think when they are out of the picture, shopping, riding, eating, in bed, in the kitchen.

There are well-fashioned characters in *The Voyage Out*. None indeed has the clarity, the robust and unique individuality of a Becky Sharp or a Dick Swiveller. But they are rounded and convincing. They move by their own vitality. Clearest of all, most certain, most inevitable in her actions, is Helen Ambrose, with her candour, her beauty, her dogmatism, her eccentric clothes, her perverse, uncompromising speech, her rudeness and her magnanimity. From the moment when she strides, in her long blue cloak, down to the Embankment, till the moment when she rises from Rachel's bedside, and passes out making way for Terence, she dominates the book like a presiding goddess. It is she who, irritated by ignorance and immaturity, undertakes Rachel's education ; she who encourages Hirst and Hewet to join their party ; she who consents to the river-trip ; she whose prescience foresees the coming doom, even as her reason mocks her apprehension. With the roots of her mind always fixed elsewhere, in England, with her children, she controls action, suggests relationships, and leads Rachel, unwittingly, yet not without foreboding, to her death. She is like one of Hardy's dynasts, herself the tool of fate ; she is like one of Michelangelo's sibyls, prescient but impotent.

It is she who, in the Indian village, was exposed to presentiments of disaster. It is she who saw that beneath the trivialities of tea-table conversation " great things were happening—terrible things because they were so great. Her sense of safety was shaken, as if beneath the twigs and dead leaves she had seen the movement of a snake. It seemed to her that a moment's respite was allowed, a moment's make-believe, and then again the profound and reasonless law asserted itself, moulding them all to its liking, making and destroying."

Helen Ambrose is used perhaps as the vehicle for Mrs. Woolf's own thoughts and sentiments. In her impatience with sentimentality, her intelligence, her conviction that it is better to be mature than immature, experienced rather than innocent, honest than self-deceived, in her touch of intellectual snobbery, her candid judgments and her distaste for politics, she shares many of Mrs. Woolf's own prejudices. But these are intellectual preferences. Helen's emotional reactions resemble rather those of Mrs. Ramsay in

To the Lighthouse. For she spoils her husband, letting him lean too heavily on her approbation, and despises herself for that. She enjoys the homage of St. John Hirst and all other young men who must inevitably admire her, accustomed, like Mrs. Ramsay, to adulation. Her mind is never wholly on the thing of the moment. Always part of it belongs to her children in London, as though, when the navel cord was cut, parting mother from child, a spiritual cord remained uniting them, which could not be severed.

The children are rarely mentioned, yet with consummate art Mrs. Woolf suggests their importance. Because of them, all London quivers before Helen through a film of tears. The thought of them for a moment warms her to Mrs. Dalloway, whom otherwise she despises as a shallow, thimble-pated chatterer. The coming of the mail excites her with knowledge that now she will know whether they are well or ill. When irritated by Rachel's changing moods and depressed by her own formless presentiments, she insists on thinking of how even at that moment her children may lie dead. And at the end, as Rachel lies dying, we see her in one last pose of extraordinary significance. The passage describing it is quiet enough.

Rachel is ill. Terence and St. John and Ridley wait at the villa. The doctor calls and leaves. Visitors from the hotel come and go. Mrs. Chailey, the housekeeper, takes charge of the watchers, bullying the household with benign familiarity.

" The afternoon, being thus shortened, passed more

quickly than they had expected. Once Mrs. Flushing opened the door, but on seeing them shut it again quickly ; once Helen came down to fetch something, but she stopped as she left the room to look at a letter addressed to her. She stood for a moment turning it over, and the extraordinary and mournful beauty of her attitude struck Terence in the way things struck him now—as something to be put away in his mind and to be thought about afterwards."

It seems very simple, yet, as Mrs. Woolf herself says of a passage in *The Watsons*, " the whole weight of the book is behind it." Helen has done all she can, of good or ill, for Rachel. Her benevolence and her wisdom can avail no longer. Her will returns to its natural element. Her mind looks back to its resting-place with her children. For although there is no mention of children in this chapter, it is by letter that she has always heard of them. The natural mother returns to her own business. Her work for her adopted child is at its end.

No other figure in the book has quite the significance of Helen's. Rachel's developing youth is beautifully drawn, but she herself is difficult to recapture, though her shyness, her inarticulateness, her blundering efforts after knowledge and self-expression are all convincing. Her reactions to Richard Dalloway's casual kiss, the awakening of her real love for Terence, her music, her moods, her unformed and irregular intelligence have been observed and are described with justice and delicacy. Moreover, they are organic. She really grows before our eyes. When she sits waiting for the tea-party which is to celebrate her engagement with Terence, she is no longer the same girl who stood arranging forks in the ship's cabin, awaiting apprehensively her aunt and uncle. " She felt herself amazingly secure . . . and able to review not only the night of the dance, but the entire past, tenderly and humorously, as if she had been turning in a fog for a long time and now could see exactly where she had turned. For the methods by which she had reached her present position seemed to her very strange, and the strangest thing about them was that she had not known where they were leading her. That was the strange thing, that one did not know where one was going, or what one wanted, and followed blindly, suffering so much in secret, always unprepared and amazed and knowing nothing ; but one thing led to another, and by degrees something had formed itself out of nothing, and so one reached at last this calm, this quiet, this certainty, and it was this process that people called living." Within a few days she was dead.

Of the men, Terence and St. John alone are drawn in full, Terence the would-be novelist, imaginative, humorous, sociable, popular, kind, inclined to be stout, surveying the world benevolently through his spectacles, untried by conflict, but not without qualities of courage and generosity. St. John Hirst is more interesting, and it is significant that Helen Ambrose should find him so. Mrs. Woolf has clearly enjoyed creating his ugly scholar's body, his fine honest mind, his temperament warped by incapacity for human

contacts, yet ennobled by moments of generous
imagination, as when he stops Rachel and Terence and
stiffly informs them that love explains everything.
She has enjoyed his vanities, his constant preoccupation
with his career, his eternal question, should he go to
the Bar or stay at Cambridge? She has made him
a butt for all the friendly laughter she bestows on
solemn young men, so earnest about their careers,
liking him, all the same, for his honesty and ability.

She even likes Ridley Ambrose a little, showing how
Rachel Vinrace found him attractive, and how his wife
could love him. But his eccentricities, his verses
shouted as he strides up and down the Embankment,
his egotism, his fussiness about comfort, his obsession with his own reputation, are mercilessly
exposed.

" For some reason the mention of letters always made
Ridley groan, and the rest of the meal passed in a
brisk argument between husband and wife as to
whether he was or was not wholly ignored by the entire
civilised world.

" ' Considering the last batch,' said Helen, ' you
deserve beating. You were asked to lecture, you
were offered a degree, and some silly woman praised
not only your books but your beauty. . . .'

" . . . He stood over the fire gazing into the depths
of the looking-glass and compressing his face into the
likeness of a commander surveying a field of battle, or
a martyr watching the flames lick his toes, rather than
that of a secluded Professor."

This, with a few words' difference, is Mr. Ramsay in

To the Lighthouse, the same tricks, the same vanities, and the same fundamental nobility.

Apart from these five, the characters are more slightly sketched. Mrs. Flushing, with her slang, her painting, her outrageous clothes, her great connections ; Miss Allan, with her suffrage badge and sensible square shoes ; Evelyn M. ; Susan Warrington ; old Mrs. Paley—they are lightly and amusingly done, with sure, quick touches. Mrs. Woolf understands how to suggest Mrs. Elliot in a conversation, or to give a hint of the sturdy independence and pathos behind Mrs. Paley's egotism. But they are minor characters, introduced to provide a social background for Rachel's evolution.

Introduced also, it seems, for another purpose. Mrs. Woolf has her standards. She is concerned with morality. She is not a moralist with the fierce caustic disgusts of Aldous Huxley ; she is not angry ; she does not preach. But she is quite certain that some characteristics are desirable and others evil. She does justice to the courage and vitality of Evelyn M., but she makes perfectly clear her low opinion of the girl's sensationalism, her cheapness, her vulgarity. She is not absolutely successful in drawing Evelyn M., the character, because she is not really at home with vulgarity. She cannot anticipate the words, appreciate the sensations of the slightly common, as she can of finer personalities. So that, as character-creation, Evelyn is far less clear and inevitable than Helen or Rachel. But as a criticism of standards she is superb. Her last scene with Mr. Perrott, when she promises to write from Moscow, is admirably done. Here is enthusiasm without proportion, vitality without judgment, egotism without dignity—all the qualities which, one suspects, Mrs. Woolf finds particularly detestable. It is clear that she worships the intellectual virtues of intelligence and honesty ; that she thinks amiability overrated, and despises self-deception. Helen's scheme for the education of Rachel is significant. " Talk was the medicine she trusted to, talk about everything, talk that was free, unguarded, and as candid as a habit of talking with men made natural in her own case. Nor did she encourage those habits of unselfishness and amiability founded upon insecurity which are put at so high a value in mixed households of men and women." These domestic virtues, indeed, are not only condemned by Mrs. Ambrose, but embodied and held up to gently devastating ridicule in the person of Susan Warrington. In Susan's monologue at tea, during the boring Sunday spent by Rachel at the hotel, lies the criticism of an entire social code.

" Both Rachel and Evelyn then began to listen to what Susan was saying.

" ' There's the ordering and the dogs and the garden, and the children coming to be taught,' her voice proceeded rhythmically as if checking the list, ' and my tennis, and the village, and letters to write for my father, and a thousand little things that don't sound much ; but I never have a moment to myself, and when I go to bed, I'm so sleepy I'm off before my head touches the pillow. Besides I like to be a great

deal with my Aunts—I'm a great bore, aren't I, Aunt
Emma ? ' (she smiled at old Mrs. Paley, who with head
slightly drooped was regarding the cake with specu-
lative affection,) ' and father has to be very careful
about chills in winter, which means a great deal of
running about, because he won't look after himself,
any more than you will, Arthur ! So it all mounts
up ! '

" Her voice mounted too, in a mild ecstasy of
satisfaction with her life and her own nature. Rachel
suddenly took a violent dislike to Susan, ignoring all
that was kindly, modest and even pathetic about
her."

Mrs. Woolf does not ignore kindliness and pathos,
but she condemns the code which imposed insincerity
upon women ; which never gave them a moment to
themselves ; which made it possible for them to be
contented with futility. She was to return to the attack
in *Night and Day* and *A Room of One's Own*. Meanwhile, she drew Susan Warrington and left it at that.

But she shows other ethical decisions as important.
When St. John Hirst swallows his pride and bitterness
and tells Hewet and Rachel that what matters is love ;
when Helen overcomes her perversity and consents to
the river-trip, these victories of generosity and benevolence are shown to be decisive, though no human
virtue can deflect the blows of fate. It is her particular philosophy to show that goodness in itself is
what matters, but that it cannot alter human destiny.
Helen was right to consent to the river-trip ; but
Rachel possibly died of its effects all the same. Fate

is certain ; death is certain ; but the courage and nobility of men and women matter more than these.

There is a third manner, however, in which character can be treated by the novelist. Mrs. Woolf not only creates characters and criticises moral values ; she creates moments. This, indeed, is her peculiar talent. She can draw all nature, all time, all human emotion into the conspiracy, all that has gone before in her book, and all that follows after, so that, looking back, the reader is given an impression of deepened significance and profundity which adjusts the balance and perspective of her whole design. In such moments wind and wave obey her ; the tropical forest, the deserted house are subdued to serve her purpose. They themselves become emanations of a mood, an anguish, an ecstasy.

When Helen and Rachel peer through the lighted windows of the hotel ; when Terence spies on them from the villa garden ; the sight of the fireworks on the return from the picnic ; the night on the river ; Helen in the native village, and the whole of Rachel's illness are moments which borrow their significance from every art and association she can give them. We feel of them, " Yes ; this is true. Yes ; life is like that."

It is done partly by a rare understanding of what human beings feel, founded on absolute loyalty to experience, and partly by a technique of writing through which she gives to commonplace parts of the action, or persons in the story, the force of symbols.

There is, for instance, the case of Nurse McInnis.

Rachel first sees her in the hotel chapel during that disastrous service when she finally abandons her churchmanship. Nurse McInnis, indeed, is the unconscious agent of that apostasy, for when Rachel watches her, she comes to the conclusion that her look of satisfaction is produced " by no splendid conception of God within her. . . . She was adoring something shallow and smug, clinging to it, so the obstinate mouth witnessed, with the assiduity of a limpet ; nothing would tear her from her demure belief in her own virtue and the virtues of her religion. . . . The face of this single worshipper became printed on Rachel's mind with an impression of keen horror, and she had it suddenly revealed to her what Helen meant and St. John meant when they proclaimed their hatred of Christianity."

When, later, she explodes to Mrs. Flushing, Nurse McInnis takes her place in the catalogue of atrocities. " ' How can they—how dare they—what do they mean by it—Mr. Bax, hospital nurses, old men, prostitutes, disgusting—— ' "

And when she falls ill and lies in a confused nightmare, it is Nurse McInnis whom Helen brings to her bedside. " And the nurse smiled steadily as they all did, and said that she did not find many people who were frightened of her."

More and more sinister she grows, without a doubt being cast upon her competence or good will. " Rachel woke to find herself in the midst of one of those interminable nights which do not end at twelve but go on into the double figures—thirteen, fourteen, and so on until they reach the twenties, and then the thirties, and then the forties. She realised that there is nothing to prevent nights from doing this if they choose. At a great distance an elderly woman sat with her head bent down ; Rachel raised herself slightly and saw with dismay that she was playing cards by the light of a candle which stood in the hollow of a newspaper. The sight had something inexplicably sinister about it, and she was terrified and cried out."

This unconscious influence passes from Rachel to Terence. After a long, anxious week, he stands one night by the window. " The lights were coming out one after another in the town beneath, and it was very peaceful and cool in the garden, so that he stepped out on to the terrace. As he stood there . . . he was overcome by a desire to escape, to have done with suffering, to forget that Rachel was ill. He allowed himself to lapse into forgetfulness of everything. As if a wind that had been raging incessantly suddenly fell asleep, the fret and strain and anxiety which had been pressing on him passed away." But his distress returns. " He remembered everything, the hour, the minute even, what point they had reached, and what was to come. . . . At last there was a rustling on the stairs, and Nurse McInnis came down fastening the links in her cuffs in preparation for the night's watch. Terence rose and stopped her . . . ' Nurse, Nurse,' he whispered, ' please tell me your opinion. Do you consider that she is very seriously ill ? Is she in any danger ? ' "

Nurse McInnis answers cautiously, professionally. She says that the case is serious. She says that they all are doing their best. But she realises that she does not satisfy Terence. " ' If you ask me,' she began in a curiously stealthy tone, ' I never like May for my patients.' "

" ' May ? ' Terence repeated.

" ' It may be a fancy, but I don't like to see anybody fall ill in May,' she continued. . . . He looked at her, but he could not answer her ; like all the others, when one looked at her she seemed to shrivel beneath one's eyes and became worthless, malicious, and untrustworthy. She slipped past him and disappeared."

Then, when he goes back to his room the whole trouble of Rachel's illness comes upon him. The cypresses, the natives, the nurse, the doctor seemed to be in a conspiracy against him with the terrible force of the illness itself. " They seemed to join together in their effort to extract the greatest possible amount of suffering from him. He could not get used to his pain, it was a revelation to him. He had never realised before that under every action, underneath the life of every day, pain lies, quiescent, but ready to devour ; he seemed to be able to see suffering, as if it were a fire, curling up over the edges of all action, eating away the lives of men and women. He thought for the first time with understanding of words which had before seemed to him empty ; the struggle of life ; the hardness of life. Now he knew for himself that life is hard and full of suffering. It seemed to him as he looked back that their happiness had never been so great as his pain was now. It had been fragmentary and incomplete, because they were so young and had not known what they were doing."

The anguish of anxiety has been drawn before by novelists, but never better than this. The figure of the nurse becomes a symbol of something sinister and inevitable in ill-health.

The emotions with which the novel deals are quite simple emotions : love, fear, boredom, anxiety, the commonplaces of human intercourse. But by her art of relating one passage in the book to another, one character to another, Mrs. Woolf gets her effect of homely and yet universal reality. It is an effect most deliberately conceived.

In *The Voyage Out* she is only beginning to develop the technique of it, but the intention is already there. It is the method of conceiving and writing her novels as a whole, so that every detail of landscape, furniture or dialogue falls into its place in the design and assumes the double significance of story and of symbol. In the later novels, especially in *To the Lighthouse* and *The Waves*, this grows clearer ; but in *The Voyage Out* it is clear enough.

Metaphor entwines itself with fact. Rachel sails away on a voyage with Ridley and Helen because a girl's education for life is an adventure, and the ultimate harbour is death as well as life. The strangeness, the isolation, the hazard of Santa Marina are all part of the design. The changing frieze of the background, from London to the sea, from the sea to South America, the river, garden, villa and hotel tell their own story. Almost without the aid of human characters, they could suggest a spiritual adventure. The mixture of wildness and domesticity is characteristic. If Joseph Conrad was Mrs. Woolf's master on the high seas, Jane Austen presided over her tea-parties. Yet the combination of their diverse influences is hers alone. She knows her limitations. If she sends Rachel to South America, she takes care to set her hotel close to the villa, so that the gentle comedy of manners may be played on the fringe of the jungle. No ferocity lurks in her forest. Her travellers encounter no wild beasts. They are not even bitten by mosquitoes. Rachel's fever might have been contracted in West Kensington. The South American landscape is taken (consciously or unconsciously) straight out of Sir Walter Raleigh's *Discovery of Guiana*. Here is Sir Walter : " On both sides this river we passed the most beautiful country that ever mine eyes beheld ; and whereas all that we had seen before was nothing but woods, prickles, bushes and thorns, here we beheld plains of twenty miles in length, the grass short and green, and in divers parts groves of trees by themselves, as if they had by all the art and labour in the world been so made of purpose ; and still as we rowed the deer came down feeding by the water's side, as if they had been used to a keeper's call."

And here is Mrs. Woolf :

" They had grown so accustomed to the wall of trees on either side that they looked up with a start when the light suddenly widened out and the trees came to an end.

78

" ' It almost reminds one of an English park,' said Mr. Flushing.

" Indeed, no change could have been greater. On both banks of the river lay an open lawn-like space, grass covered and planted, for the gentleness and order of the place suggested human care, with graceful trees at the top of little mounds. As far as they could gaze, this lawn rose and sank with the undulating motion of an old English park.

" ' It might be Arundel or Windsor,' Mr. Flushing continued, ' if you cut down that bush with the yellow flowers ; and, by Jove, look ! '

" Rows of brown backs paused for a moment and then leapt with a motion as if they were springing over waves out of sight. For a moment no one of them could believe that they had really seen live animals in the open—a herd of wild deer, and the sight aroused a childlike excitement in them, dissipating their gloom."

The plagiarism is as justifiable as Shakespeare's. Mrs. Woolf's business is with the human spirit ; she can borrow her geographical background from whom she pleases. Her rivers and cities are symbols, not natural curiosities to be described from first-hand evidence for their own sake.

But the significance with which she can endow them is extraordinary. The moth in the hotel, after Rachel's death, becomes a tragic and sinister presence. The hotel guests become themselves figures of human reality and indifference. Their procession past St. John Hirst as one by one they gathered up books, cards and work-baskets and went upstairs to bed, is a procession of life closing in upon death, of the inexorable march of human destiny.

To have one's vision, to see the pattern, to know, to understand—that is the purpose of life, the satisfaction permitted to her characters, even in this first novel. Its philosophy, its theme and its spirit unite it with her later work. But here she has curbed her fancy, and accepted the traditional novel-form. She plays no tricks with time. Night follows day ; the invitation precedes the party ; the families are duly labelled marked, and assigned to their proper station in Society. If later Mrs. Woolf was to abandon the tools inherited from her predecessors and to throw them out of the window, it was not because she could not handle them with ease and mastery. The artistic sobriety and perfection of *The Voyage Out* gave her the right to be a rebel ; for it proved that she could have remained with complete success within the convention had she chosen to do so.

IV
VIRGINIA WOOLF IS NOT JANE AUSTEN

The Voyage Out was well received. It is true that the war was in progress, that few people were taking much interest in literature, and that the temper of the book was singularly remote from the circumstances of the time. But those who encountered it, applauded. *The Spectator* declared it to be " that rarest of things, a novel of serious artistic value." E. M. Forster praised its fearlessness, its assurance, its unity. The *Observer*, the *Pall Mall Gazette*, the *Manchester Guardian*, the *Standard*, *The Field* and *The Queen* acclaimed it. If its qualities were quiet rather than spectacular, they were not obscure. The novel had beauty, profundity, observation and intelligence. If it was based on limited experience, its spirit was unafraid. If Mrs. Woolf lacked the physical vitality and practical knowledge of Dickens, Tolstoi, Balsac, Fielding or Victor Hugo, if she never rose to the passion of Emily Brontë, she had poetry and humour ; she was master in her own kingdom, and her mastery was recognised.

This was encouraging. Whatever handicaps might beset her in writing her second novel, the discouragement of which comes from lack of recognition by intelligent and discerning critics was not hers.

She had, however, other disadvantages. She was ill. At the time of writing her second novel she was allowed to work for only about an hour a day, a maddening restriction for a writer. This is probably the reason why the book is much too long, as though in determining not to be beaten by her illness she had driven herself to write too much.

Then, too, the oppression of the war must have been terrific. She has given little direct indication of its effect upon her, but into almost all the work she wrote after 1919 she introduces some reference to it, as though its memory were the scar of an old wound she could not hide.

The cry of "War! War! War! Declaration of War!" breaks in upon the arguments of Jane and Elizabeth and Poll in *A Society*. In *Kew Gardens* the elderly gentleman observes to his attendant, "Heaven was known to the ancients as Thessaly, William, and now, with this war, the spirit matter is rolling between the hills like thunder." The inconsequent meditations in *The Mark on the Wall* are interrupted by " Someone is standing over me and saying—

" ' I'm going out to buy a newspaper.'

" ' Yes ? '

" ' Though it's no good buying newspapers. . . . Nothing ever happens. Curse this War! God damn this War ! ' " In *The String Quartette* we learn that Regent Street is up and the Treaty signed. *Jacob's Room* is, in its way, Mrs. Woolf's "war book."

The war has happened, and nothing is ever quite the same again. We are allowed to see its effects, not its action, as the Greeks kept their murders and violence off-stage. But she only wrote of the war when it was over. In *Night and Day* she deliberately shut it out.

Now Jane Austen, whose brothers were sailors and whose social contacts were largely with the families of army or naval officers, wrote during the war against Napoleon and contrived with complete success to exclude it from her novels. The French Revolution, the Second and Third Coalitions, the Battles of the Nile, Trafalgar and Waterloo leave little mark on *Pride and Prejudice* or *Emma*. It is true that in *Persuasion* Anne Elliott thinks tenderly of the hardship and insecurity of a sailor's life, and the Peace meant an added facility in letting Kellynch Hall to a rich naval officer. But Mr. Bennett, Mrs. Dashwood and Emma Woodhouse could go their way through her novels without concern for the heroism of Sir John Moore, or Pitt's attempt to suppress the " Friends of the Revolution," because in real life this exclusion actually was possible. In that period of slow communications and social isolation middle-class England was probably as little affected by political events as Jane Austen showed it to have been.

But the England of 1918 was not the England of 1818. Virginia Woolf was not Jane Austen. The difficulty of a novelist during the twentieth-century war lay in its all-pervading influence. It affected every personal as well as every impersonal problem. To increase the difficulty, it transferred interest from immediate events to something beyond.

The events of a novel must appear important. Trivial though they may be, they must create the illusion that they fill the universe. Jane Austen was able to create the illusion that a delayed proposal or an invitation to a ball could fill the universe, because, so far as her little world was concerned, it did. But in England during the twentieth-century war no single domestic activity was without reference to that tremendous, undomestic violence. At any moment a telegram might arrive ; the sirens might signal an approaching air-raid ; somebody might come unexpectedly home on leave. The interest of every occupation, from buying groceries to writing a love-letter, was in some measure deflected to France, Egypt or Gallipoli. The closed stage, the cosy humour essential to the comedy of manners had been invaded by events and anxieties too violent for comedy.

If Mrs. Woolf wished to write a domestic story on the Jane Austen model, she had to stage its scene at a time prior to August 1914. And this she did. No dates are quoted, but from internal evidence, from the appearance of taxis, a suffrage office in Russell Square, the social claims of William Rodney, and the freedom of Mary Datchet, we can gather that the date is round about 1912.

The story is the most elaborate attempted by Mrs. Woolf. Katharine Hilbery, granddaughter of the poet, Richard Allardyce, lives with her distinguished and cultured parents in a house on Chelsea Embankment, which is partly a rendezvous for literary London and partly a museum in honour of the departed great. To a Sunday afternoon tea-party comes Ralph Denham, a young man from a large impoverished family in

Highgate, who writes articles on law for Mr. Hilbery's review ; and he immediately, devastatingly, but half-unconsciously, falls in love with Katharine. She is about to become engaged to a pedantic but wholly eligible bachelor, William Rodney, while Ralph appears to be the natural suitor of Mary Datchet, a clergyman's daughter employed in a suffrage office. After sundry meetings and partings, these four young people find themselves in Lincolnshire for Christmas—Ralph staying with Mary's family, Katharine and William, now openly engaged, at her cousins' the Otways. But when Ralph is about to propose to Mary and thus complete the expected union of the two couples, he catches sight of Katharine through the window of the inn where they are lunching, and betrays his true allegiance. From that moment, the retreat begins. Mary refuses his proposal ; William finds himself falling in love with Katharine's cousin—Cassandra Otway ; the ultimate re-arrangement is complicated and delayed by social conventions ; Katharine's own family and William's acutely developed sense of decorum delaying and at one time endangering the proper and inevitable grouping ; but finally Cassandra and William, Katharine and Ralph, are comfortably united, and Mary, if left without a partner, is compensated by the deep and abiding satisfaction of her work.

Now here is a plot completely characteristic of English domestic comedy, subject to all its limitations. The action is confined to the polite behaviour of well-bred, well-to-do people behaving suitably within the conventions of their social code. No one is very rich in the book, nor, for all Ralph's anxieties, is anyone very poor. The only scandal takes place off-stage, and is referred to in hushed whispers or mentioned in letters. The couples advance and retreat with the urbane decorum of dancers in a minuet. No one behaves badly; no villainies are discovered; no accidents intrude upon the smooth development of the story. All forms of violent passion are excluded; wickedness, pain, and even extreme anxiety have no place here. It is the only one of Mrs. Woolf's novels, except *Orlando*, in which death plays no decisive part. If there are moments of drama and apprehension, these concern moral decisions rather than the anguish of conflict or the excitement of physical danger. The unities of time and place are observed. No one goes farther afield than Lincolnshire, and even there, the climate is so gently tempered that roses bloom, without evoking comment, at Christmas time, in the Rectory garden.

Nothing in the novel transcends tradition. The actions are recognisable and familiar. Those delicate gradations of thought, those subtle sequences of reference, the interplay of symbol with fact, which contribute so much to Mrs. Woolf's later novels, cannot be found here. It is as though, feeling herself restricted by illness and by circumstance, she decided to make a virtue of necessity, and to bind her imagination in the tight ligatures of Austenian comedy.

It is, indeed, precisely the type of plot which Jane Austen might have chosen. It was within similar restrictions that she had moved so happily. In her essay *On Not Knowing Greek*, Mrs. Woolf described the danger and possibilities of that position, drawing her audacious parallel between Jane Austen and Sophocles. Commenting on the *Electra*, she writes : " Of that, in spite of our weakness and distortion, what remains to us ? That his genius was of the extreme kind in the first place ; that he chose a design which, if it failed, would show its failure in gashes and ruin, not in the gentle blurring of some insignificant detail, which if it succeeded would cut every stroke to the bone, would stamp each finger-print in marble. . . . It is thus, with a thousand differences of degree, that in English literature Jane Austen shapes a novel. . . . In Jane Austen, too, we have the same sense, though the ligatures are much less tight, that her figures are bound, and restricted to a few definite movements. She too, in her modest everyday prose, chose the dangerous art where one slip means death."

Mrs. Woolf, in *Night and Day*, chose it and failed. It is not so much that in any place one can point to the slip which has meant death. Nor is the novel dead. It has beauty and gravity, nobility of theme and high distinction. But, in the first place, Jane Austen was not the master for Mrs. Woolf to follow. She admired and understood her. In 1919 it is highly probable that she understood Jane Austen better than she understood herself. She appreciated Jane Austen's perfection, her integrity, her technical skill and her exquisite discrimination of moral values. To a large extent, she shared these. There is the incident where Ralph takes Katharine to tea at his home in Highgate, which with its apparent superficiality, and its real profundity of spiritual insight, is just the kind of thing Jane Austen did so perfectly ; and Mrs. Woolf does it very well. She makes us feel, as Jane Austen makes us feel in *The Watsons* when Lord Osborne comes to call, " as if we had been made witness of a matter of the highest importance." But this is not really Mrs. Woolf's true *genre*. Her technique is the technique of experiment, not of tradition. Her hunting-ground lies among the subtle gradations of sentiment, memory and association to which less delicate sight is blind. She was, in *Night and Day*, playing a game which was a good game, which had once been played almost perfectly, which she could play better than most ; but it was not her game. She was a disciple here, not a master ; a follower, not a maker of the law.

There was another mistake. *Night and Day* is, from one point of view, a comedy of restrictions, and the theme, suitable though it may seem to the Austenian comedy, was, in Mrs. Woolf's hands, unsuitable. For she is, in spite of her respect for classical tradition, a rebel against restrictions. She is concerned with reality, at war with unreality ; she is concerned with true standards, at war with false ones. And in *Night and Day* false standards and unreality are bound up with the social code under which her characters live. When the novel opens, Katharine and Ralph can both live their real life only in their dreams, because in their waking life, falsity is imposed upon them. The story tells of their escape into reality, and into true values.

Now all this involves a criticism of society, and here

Mrs. Woolf differs from Jane Austen. Jane Austen laughed at snobbery and insensitiveness and ill-humour. Sir Walter Elliot was vain, Mr. Collins was "not a sensible man," Mrs. Bennett was foolish, Marianne Dashwood a goose. Within the existing framework of society, according to the best accepted standards of moral value, she moved with absolute justice and assurance. But she did not criticise the framework. She did not seek to change the standard. Anne Elliot may know her sister to be snobbish and overbearing ; she may regret her surrender to Lady Russell's over-persuasion ; but she never disputes the right of superior birth to dictate opinion, she does not complain of the tradition which doomed her, unmarried, to subordination and triviality of occupation. The cry of Florence Nightingale, imprisoned in the same sur-roundings of decorum and of comfort, that she was " starving and diseased " upon them, is never heard in the novels of Jane Austen. For Jane Austen was far from starvation and disease. Her appetites for quiet laughter, curiosity, humour and observation were amply satisfied by the circumstances of her life. The domestic activities of the middle-classes nourished them. She was never compelled to separate reverie from her waking life, for the latter provided all that she could need for the development and enrichment of her genius. It was her peculiar fortune to live at a time and in circumstances ideally suited to her talent.

But that was not true of Virginia Woolf when she set herself to compose *Night and Day*. She was too well aware that the domestic virtues, recognised as admirable by Jane Austen, were not the crown of life. Her story is shaped so that, in order to develop fully, her characters had first to discard tradition. It is this implied criticism, this straining toward some larger life, some more liberal standard of values, which disturbs the quiet and enclosed perfection of the comedy. *Night and Day* is a less perfect book than *Pride and Prejudice* or *Emma*, because its writer could no longer accept uncritically Jane Austen's world.

It is possible that no writer will ever repeat that miracle. Emily Davies, Florence Nightingale and Emmeline Pankhurst have made that impossible ; the war made it impossible ; Margaret MacDonald, Keir Hardie and Bernard Shaw made it impossible. For they have broken into the seclusion of the country vicarage, the drawing-room, the Assembly Rooms at Bath. They have ruffled the little tranquil pool of consciousness which was Jane Austen's. The assurance that was Chaucer's, that was Jane Austen's, can only be found, Mrs. Woolf herself has explained, when " the poet has made up his mind about young women, of course, but also about the world they live in, its end, its nature, and his own craft and technique, so that his mind is free to apply its force fully to its objects." But that was not the case with Mrs. Woolf. She lived at a transition period. Her world was changing under her eyes. To have made up her mind about it yesterday meant that she might be wrong to-day. In spite of her limited experience and her refusal to take sides, she was in sympathy with the rebels who were removing the old landmarks. When she wrote of women, she

wrote of a generation as adventurous in its exploration of experience as the Elizabethan men had been
in their exploration of the globe. The women whom
Mrs. Woolf knew were exploring the professional
world, the political world, the world of business, discovering that they themselves had legs as well as
wombs, brains as well as nerves, reason as well as
sensibility ; their Americas lay within themselves, and
altered the map as profoundly as any added by Cabot
or Columbus. Like Raleigh, they founded their new
colonies ; like Drake, they combined national service
with privateering. Mrs. Woolf, who had fallen in
love with the Elizabethan age, could not possibly be
blind to this one. She disliked the suffrage office, but
she hailed its ultimate effect. And the lesson her
preferences taught her was that salvation, which means
redemption from unreality, lies in freedom.

Consequently, her theme and her characters are too
big for her plot. They stretch it to breaking-point.
She chose for her heroine Katharine Hilbery, a young
woman drawn on altogether too large and heroic a
scale to sit comfortably behind the tea-tray, first in her
parents', then in her husband's house. All that Anne
Elliot needed, all that Elizabeth Bennet and Emma
Woodhouse needed, was to sit behind a tea-tray, given
the right tea-tray. Katharine Hilbery wanted much
more than that. Mrs. Woolf gave her beauty ; she
gave her composure ; she gave her the ability to conduct her parents' house and organise her mother's
work on her grandfather's biography ; but she gave
her also the heroic proportions which made these

accomplishments a prison for her real self. Thus while living with her parents, she pursued in secret the unladylike study of advanced mathematics, or tamed wild horses on imaginary prairies. Her dream life and her active life were completely alienated. It was a state of mind which proved the undoing of Madame Bovary. It is one which Freud has condemned. But it is a state of mind inevitable to those young women who, like Katharine Hilbery, lead lives directed by family tradition rather than by free choice.

Just because Katharine's active world was divorced from her dream world, she could do nothing truly. She became engaged to William Rodney, whom she did not love, in that state of partial anæsthesia in which young women leading unreal lives frequently accept proposals from eligible bachelors. All life being unreal, this is no worse than any other. If Katharine had really married William, both would have remained detached from reality until their death.

But it is typical of Mrs. Woolf that one real emotion, one absolutely true standard, should break the vicious circle. She believes in love. It was not for nothing that in *The Voyage Out* she gave to the fastidious intellectual, St. John Hirst, her profession of faith in its importance. Mary really loves Ralph, and having known love as a reality, she refuses to be satisfied with its shadow. At the moment when Ralph is about to propose to her she recognises that he loves Katharine Hilbery.

" ' Katharine Hilbery ! ' Mary thought, in an instant

of blinding revelation ; ' I've always known it was Katharine Hilbery ! ' She knew it all now.

" After a moment of downcast stupor, she raised her eyes, looked steadily at Ralph, and caught his fixed and dreamy gaze levelled at a point far beyond their surroundings, a point that she had never reached in all the time she had known him. . . . She noticed everything about him ; if there had been other signs of his utter alienation she would have sought them out too, for she felt that it was only by heaping one truth upon another that she could keep herself sitting there, upright. The truth seemed to support her ; it struck her, even as she looked at his face, that the light of truth was shining far away beyond him ; the light of truth, she seemed to frame the words as she rose to go, shines on a world not to be shaken by our personal calamities."

So, when finally on the walk home he asked her to marry him, she replied that she could not do it. Her refusal set Ralph free to pursue Katharine ; Katharine was able to release William, who loved Cassandra, and slowly, for each of them, the dream world became identified with reality, the night changed into day, the union was complete, a union not so much of a man with a woman, as of a man with himself, a woman with herself.

For one interesting thing about *Night and Day* is that in it Mrs. Woolf links the satisfaction of love with the discovery of truth. She does not disregard sexual attraction. Her novel is not that desideratum of the provincial circulating library, " a nice love-story without any sex in it." She has never shown herself in the least afraid of any aspect of human nature, and in *Jacob's Room* was to shock a little some of her readers who had mistaken her previous reticence for prudery. She is well aware that virility is attractive, but she estimated that attraction at a lower value than most.

There is a significant incident in *Night and Day* where Katharine and William, ostensibly engaged but actually estranged, walk from Lincoln back to the Otways'.

" He went on now to tell her of his love for her, in words which bore, even to her critical senses, the stamp of truth ; but none of this touched her until, coming to a gate whose hinge was rusty, he heaved it open with his shoulder. The virility of this deed impressed her ; and yet, normally, she attached no value to the power of opening gates. The strength of muscles has nothing to do on the face of it with the strength of affections ; nevertheless, she felt a sudden concern for this power running to waste on her account, which, combined with a desire to keep possession of that strangely attractive male power, made her rouse herself from her torpor."

Thus far Katharine's reactions are such as might have been found in a D. H. Lawrence heroine, though these attach, normally, considerable " value to the power of opening gates." The strength of muscles, in most Georgian and, indeed, much Edwardian fiction, has a great deal to do with the strength of the affections. But Katharine's subsequent behaviour is typical of Mrs. Woolf's young women. She is moved, and being moved by a spirit of real affection, is strong enough to tell William the truth, that she does not love him. Only his tears and his weakness, which follow her declaration, drive her back to falsity and a renewed engagement.

For the test of love in Mrs. Woolf's sense is that it makes truth possible. When Katharine walked with Ralph on the Embankment, while half of her mind listened to his confession of obsession with her and with his image of her, " she was feeling happier than she had felt in her life. If Denham could have seen how visibly books of algebraic symbols, pages all speckled with dots and dashes and twisted bars, came before her eyes as they trod the Embankment, his secret joy in her attention might have been dispersed." Real love set Katharine free to think about mathematics. Real love made it possible for her at last to bring from hiding her furtive papers. Ralph could read her secret—she could read his. And by giving herself away she discovered that " she had committed no sacrilege but enriched herself, perhaps immeasurably, perhaps eternally. She hardly dared steep herself in the infinite bliss." This is a totally different consummation of love from that in *Lady Chatterley's Lover*, but it bears about it as clearly the stamp of truth.

Katharine and Ralph, William and Cassandra, found their release in love ; but Mary Datchet, who had made possible their release, was not left unsatisfied. She sits in her room in London, alone or with a strange and quite impersonal young man, laying plans for a new political society. When Ralph and Katharine, in their happiness, go to visit her, and Ralph wishes to tell her the news of his engagement, they look up at her lighted window. " It signalled to her across the dark street ; it was a sign of triumph shining there for ever, not to be extinguished this side the grave. . . . They stood for some moments looking at the illuminated blinds, an expression to them both of something impersonal and serene in the spirit of the woman within, working out her plans far into the night—her plans for the good of a world that none of them were ever to know."

The light in the solitary spinster's room was to Mrs. Woolf a sign of triumph, not of loneliness. Her work for a world that none of them would know, might be a tedious political design perhaps, but one whose ultimate purpose, the defence of truth, the liberation of the spirit, was more important than the fortuitous satisfaction of a personal love.

Mrs. Woolf works in symbols, and it was not by accident that she chose as the agent for breaking the bonds of unreality and setting true love free, a suffrage worker. In one sense *Night and Day* is a fable of the process taking place in English society before the war, when Mrs. Fawcett and Mrs. Pankhurst were not only leading young ladies from stagnation in the quiet backwaters of their parents' homes, but were making a far more honourable and true marriage relationship possible for them.

The theme is fine ; it is characteristic ; it is perfectly suitable for a novel. But not for this novel. The texture of the comedy is too light and too complex. The whole story is too long. It lacks vitality. It contains too much social chit-chat and repetition. The characters take tea together too often, even for a drawing-room comedy. But the measure of its failure was, perhaps, a mercy. It drove Mrs. Woolf to seek new forms of expression. It marked the end of her apprenticeship to tradition.

V

"OUT OF THE WINDOW"

MAY 18, 1924, was the date on which, when reading
Mr. Bennett and Mr. Brown to the "Heretics"
Society at Cambridge, Mrs. Woolf uttered her challenge to the Edwardian tradition. She had gone to
the Edwardians, she said, asking them how to set
about the novelist's proper business of creating character. How was she to create a woman, Mrs. Brown?
"And they said, 'Begin by saying that her father
kept a shop in Harrogate. Ascertain the rent. Ascertain the wages of shop assistants in the year 1878.
Discover what her mother died of. Describe cancer.
Describe calico. Describe . . .' But I cried 'Stop!
Stop!' And I regret to say that I threw that ugly,
that clumsy, that incongruous tool out of the window,
for I knew that if I began describing the cancer and
the calico, my Mrs. Brown, that vision to which I
cling, though I know no way of imparting it to you,
would have been dulled and tarnished and vanished
for ever."

Now, although we must not take too seriously any
statement made in a paper read to a literary society for
undergraduates, the incident narrated here is not quite
fanciful. There was a time—we find it recorded in
An Unwritten Novel—when Mrs. Woolf sat opposite
an unknown woman in a railway carriage. Call her
Mrs. Brown; call her Minnie Marsh; call her

Katharine Hilbery, or Evelyn M. It does not matter. She had possessed herself of Mrs. Woolf's imagination. She was the subject of a novel. She demanded liberation into that extended reality which art alone can give. And Mrs. Woolf had gone to the Edwardians —to the Victorians too, if we must be precise—and had asked them how to deal with her. She had, in *The Voyage Out*, described a ship, described a villa, described the domestic arrangements of Helen's brother and of Mrs. Chailey. In *Night and Day* she had described the Hilberys' house, described Ralph's bedroom, described Richard Allardyce and the aunts and the correspondence about Cyril. And she was not satisfied. So she had forthwith flung the tools she had hitherto used out of the window, and had started again with an entirely new technique. In 1919 she published, as well as *Night and Day*, two little essays, *Kew Gardens* and *The Mark on the Wall*, entirely unlike anything that she had produced before. Two years later they reappeared in volume form, issued by the Hogarth Press together with several other sketches decorated with woodcuts by Vanessa Bell, bearing the title *Monday or Tuesday*.

The fascination of that little book lies largely in the knowledge of what went before and what was to follow after.

In it Mrs. Woolf was experimenting, stretching her prose to the fullest limits of intelligibility, and sometimes beyond, seeing how far it was possible to discard description, discard narrative, discard the link-sentences which bind ideas together, seeing how far it was possible to write her prose from within, like poetry, giving it a life of its own. She was devising her new technique ; she was testing possibilities and discovering her own powers. And what is particularly interesting about *Monday or Tuesday* is that it contains, as in an artist's sketch-book, brief designs and lightly traced outlines of each of the experimental styles, and even of the manners of thought, which Mrs. Woolf was to develop in that sequence of novels which leads from *Jacob's Room* to *The Waves*.

If Mrs. Woolf used a technique sometimes employed by Joyce, she did not copy him. She produced *The Mark on the Wall* and *Kew Gardens* in 1919. He published *Ulysses* in 1922 and though it is true that parts had appeared earlier in *The Little Review*, there is no evidence that Mrs. Woolf read them there. If some of her subsequent modes of thought resembled those of Proust, she did not copy Proust, interested in him though she undoubtedly is. According to M. Delattre, who seems to know, she did not read Proust till 1922.

And by 1919 she had begun to question the necessity of all the heavy impedimenta of plot, narrative and description hindering the novelist. Why, she seems to have asked herself, should he be weighed down by all the external trappings of life ? (They had, indeed, weighed her down in *Night and Day*.) It is all so long, so cumbrous, so unnecessary ; why should we pander to the stupidity of readers, who might perhaps be induced to take these matters for granted ? Poets, after all, do it. Poets present sensations, emotions and processes of thought, with only lightly indicated backgrounds. They reveal, rather than explain. They suggest. They illumine. They flash a torch through the darkness on to a child's green bucket, an aster trembling violently in the wind, or blades of grass bent by the rain, and leave us to imagine the wild storm-swept garden, and the children safely tucked in bed for the night. Poets have immense advantages over novelists.

In one essay, *Notes on an Elizabethan Play*, now published in *The Common Reader*, Mrs. Woolf draws her comparison between Ford's and Tolstoi's tragedies, between the poetical drama and the prose novel. " Then, at once, the prime differences emerge ; the long leisurely accumulated novel ; the little contracted play ; the emotion all split up, dissipated, and then woven together, slowly and gradually massed into a whole, in the novel ; the emotion concentrated, generalised, heightened in the play. What moments of intensity, what phrases of astonishing beauty the play shot at us !

" O, my lords,
I but deceived your eyes with antic gesture,
When one news straight came huddling on another
Of death ! and death ! and death ! still I danced forward."

Or

" You have oft for these two lips
Neglected cassia or the natural sweets
Of the spring violet ; they are not yet much withered."

With all her reality, Anna Karenina could never say

> " You have oft for these two lips
> Neglected cassia ! "

Some of the most profound of human emotions are
therefore beyond her reach. The extremes of passion
are not for the novelist ; the perfect marriage of sense
and sound are not for him ; he must turn his swiftness
to sluggardry ; keep his eyes on the ground, not on
the sky ; suggest by description, not reveal by illu-
mination. Instead of singing—

> " Lay a garland on my hearse
> Of the dismal yew ;
> Maidens willow branches bear :
> Say I died true,"

we must enumerate the chrysanthemums fading on the
grave and the undertakers' men snuffling past in their
four-wheelers. How, then, can we compare this
lumbering and lagging art with poetry ? "

Mrs. Woolf, the critic, did compare it, and found
that *Anna Karenina* came off after all not so badly
in the comparison, and that *War and Peace* remained
a great book. But Mrs. Woolf the artist would not
let well alone. Why, indeed, should novelists resign
themselves to their disadvantages ? Why should they
leave so much to the poets ?

She did not want to write verse. She wanted to
write prose. In 1920 she published in *The Athenæum*
a review of an anthology of English prose in which she
states her prejudice. " But no, I dare not breathe a
word against English poetry. All I will venture is a
sigh of wonder and amazement that when there is

prose before us with its capacities and possibilities, its power to say new things, make new shapes, suggest new passions, young people should still be dancing to a barrel-organ and choosing words because they rhyme." It is plain that her mind was busy with the teasing subject. Twelve years later, in her *Letter to a Young Poet*, she declares that her practice of writing prose has bred in her " a foolish jealousy " of poets. She wished to eat her cake and have it, to write prose while enjoying the freedoms of the poet.

In *Monday or Tuesday* we see her experimenting to see how it would work. The first sketch included in the volume, " A Haunted House," is pure poetry. It presents pictures ; it reveals a mood ; it unites sense and sound ; it eliminates all the external facts demanded by conventional prose ; it suggests instead of describing, and it is written with a cadence which only just escapes being pure *vers libre*.

In a way, that is nothing new. Novelists have often slipped into something near the rhythm of poetry in moments of excitement. Dickens had done it— disastrously ; Mrs. Woolf had, in an essay, defended Meredith for doing it. But neither the death of Little Nell, nor the meeting between Richard Feverel and Lucy, has quite the silvery, ethereal, de-la-Mareish music of *A Haunted House*. The sentences suggest irresistibly a verse arrangement.

> " A moment later the light had faded.
> Out in the garden then.
> But the trees spun darkness
> For a wandering beam of sun.

So fine, so rare,
Coolly sunk beneath the surface
The beam I sought always burnt behind the glass.
Death was the glass ;
Death was between us ;
Coming to the woman first, hundreds of years ago,
Leaving the house,
Sealing all the windows ;
The rooms were darkened.
He left it, left her,
Went North, went East,
Saw the stars turned in the Southern sky ;
Sought the house, found it
Dropped beneath the Downs.
' Safe, safe, safe,' the pulse of the house beat gladly,
' The treasure yours.' "

Ezra Pound, Anne Wickham, or Richard Aldington would certainly not have written that as prose ; they might easily have written something very similar as verse.

But music and cadence are not the only gifts of poetry that Mrs. Woolf would borrow. There is the use of elimination, omitting descriptive and narrative facts, and relying on the reader's imagination to supply them. Why not set picture beside picture, phrase by phrase, as in a poem, and let their juxtaposition, unexplained, form its own meaning? Music does that ; poetry does that. Why not prose ? It was, on the whole, a more audacious innovation than the experiment with cadence. In each of these sketches she does it to some extent, but the most complete form of it is in *The String Quartette*.

There is the colloquial opening : " Well, here we

are, and if you cast your eye over the room you will
see that tubes and trams and omnibuses, private
carriages not a few, even, I venture to believe, landaus
with bays in them, have been busy at it, weaving
threads from one end of London to the other. . . ."
Then someone is saying that Regent Street is up,
and the Treaty signed, and a word about the weather,
and the memory darts back to the domestic tragedy
of having forgotten to write about a leak in the larder ;
then forward to a relative now met after seven years.
It becomes clear that Mrs. Woolf is at a concert,
sitting with a hundred or so members of an audience,
passive on gilt chairs, waiting for the music to begin.
But we have to deduce for ourselves which are the
thoughts in her mind, which the half-buried memories,
which the words of her neighbours, and which the
images suggested by the early Mozart quartette.
" The tongue is but a clapper. Simplicity itself.
The feathers in the hat next me are bright and
pleasing as a child's rattle. The leaf on the plane-
tree flashes green through the chink in the curtain.
Very strange, very exciting.

' How — how — how ! ' Hush !
These are the lovers on the grass."

It is the picture of a concert ; it is a poem about music,
about one individual's response to music ; with a
light sketching of figures, as though by Monet in his
early work, their outlines dim, their attitudes significant. There is no doubt that it is effective, though
odd and teasing as a poem by Edith Sitwell. Difficult,

delicate, requiring a touch so light and firm that only a brave artist would attempt it ; a daring method, exposed to the complementary dangers of violence and weakness ; but holding out entrancing possibilities.

Reading through the sketches, we come upon another trait. Here is a passage from *The Mark on the Wall* : " I like to think of the tree itself : first the close dry sensation of being wood ; then the grinding of the storm ; then the slow delicious ooze of sap. . . . The song of birds must sound very loud and strange in June ; and how cold the feet of insects must feel upon it, as they make laborious progresses up the creases of the bark, or sun themselves upon the thin green awning of the leaves, and look straight in front of them with diamond-cut red eyes. . . ." " How cold the feet of insects must feel. . . ." There is a comparable passage in *Kew Gardens* describing the light falling down through a flower-bed on to the smooth grey back of a pebble, the shell of a snail, or a raindrop. Such minute yet intense perception, such sympathetic intimacy with non-human objects, feeling the cold feet of insects, or the light expanding in a rain-drop, such close identification of the emotion of the beholder with the thing perceived, belong to poetry rather than prose, or to the more delicate forms of decorative art. They require an observation as minutely accurate as it is imaginative, and a sense of the unity of all manifestations of life which dwells in the metaphors of the poets. To think oneself into the sensations of a tree or a stone is a poet's or painter's privilege. For a prose-writer it has its obvious dangers. Balance is hard enough to achieve at any time : with the world so large, and wars and empires and trade slumps and engineering so active, it is difficult to disentangle the small personal affairs of Mr. Brown and Mrs. James. If we are to involve ourselves also in the sensations of trees and snails, where will it end ? Jane Austen kept her observation quietly to the comedy of individual, decorous, middle-class men and women. Tolstoi moved among wars and empires ; Dostoievsky ranged through Heaven and Hell and all the disorders of the human spirit. And here is Mrs. Woolf applying an exquisite and microscopic observation to the cold feet of insects. Certainly this is making an unusual demand on the novelist, complacently blind as a rule to anything smaller than a handbag, a parasol, or the hatpins so dramatically used by Anatole France's wayward heroines. But there is no reason, of course, why his field of observation should be so limited.

The use of cadence, of elimination, of a microscopic observation, might have been enough for a less experimental writer. But there was another practice which Mrs. Woolf did not originate, but at which she was anxious to try her hand. Dorothy Richardson did not invent the " stream of consciousness " technique, but she had re-introduced it ; she had made people talk about it. In March 1919 Duckworth—the firm which also published *Night and Day*, the firm with which Mrs. Woolf was connected by relationship—published *The Tunnel*. It was not quite new, resembling something in Sterne, and something in

Proust. It is probable that Mrs. Woolf had read Dorothy Richardson ; it is certain that she had read Sterne ; if M. Delattre is right, she had not yet read *Du Côté de chez Swann*, which had been published by Bernard Grasset in 1913, fell flat, and was not heard of much until, four years later, in the middle of the war, *La Nouvelle Revue Française* called attention to its remarkable quality. It does not seem important. At certain times particular forms of style present themselves to different writers, and quite independently of each other they begin to work on similar lines ; just as scientific theories or mechanical inventions seem from time to time to blow about the world waiting for receptive minds to catch and fertilise them. So Bleriot laid a wreath on the grave of the aeroplane-designer, Bondfield ; so the theory of the circulation of the blood presented itself to different scientists almost simultaneously.

To lie still and let sensations, suggestions, thoughts stream through the mind, to attempt no arbitrary control, but to analyse and record the contents of the flowing river, as analysts record the nature of Thames water, that is an activity likely to attract writers of the generation that intellectually discovered the subconscious and invented the technique of free association.

Kew Gardens and *The Mark on the Wall* are both exercises in free association, with this difference. In *The Mark on the Wall* Mrs. Woolf shows herself sitting in winter time before the fire, smoking a cigarette after tea, and letting her eye rest on the burning coals, the chrysanthemums in the round glass bowl, and on the mark on the wall. As she watches it, she thinks of a crimson flag flapping from a castle town, of ants bearing a blade of straw, the people who lived in the house before she did, the mystery of life, odd things one loses, immortality (at which she thinks herself as small as Hans Andersen's Thumberlina, so that the cup of a flower, as it turns over, deluges her with purple and red light), the dust which buried Troy, Shakespeare, thoughts that are pleasant because flattering to ourselves, flowers, the looking-glasses through which we look at life, followed by a very important speculation on the novelists of the future, followed by an indictment of generalisations, and boring masculine standards, of Sunday walks and Whitaker's Table of Precedency, followed by a thought that the mark may be a tumulus, which leads on to antiquaries and learned men in general, and an ideal world without specialists or superstitions ; then a reflection on nature's game of prompting us to action as a remedy for painful thoughts, then on other remedies—thoughts of the impersonal world, a chest of drawers, wood, the trees from which wood comes, the fate of trees . . . suddenly there is interruption. Somebody stands over her, saying :

" ' I'm going out to buy a newspaper.'

" ' Yes ? '

" ' Though it's no good buying newspapers. . . . Nothing ever happens. Curse this war ! God damn this war ! . . . All the same, I don't see why we should have a snail on our wall.'

" Ah, the mark on the wall ! It was a snail ! "

Now though that seems, when summarised, to be an incoherent jumble of irrelevant reflections, in the essay itself each idea leads naturally from the other, somewhat after the fashion of those strings of words with which Mr. Pelman begins his memory-training courses. It is no less coherent than the " Argument " printed above a long eighteenth-century poem. And unpromising though the material may seem, the combined result has beauty. It derives unity from Mrs. Woolf's own consciousness. Her mind holds it together. There she lies, all the time, in her chair beside the fire, till interrupted by that sharp, dramatic violence. The external moment rushes with fierce impact upon the flowing thought. She is in the present world. It is war-time. Somebody wants to buy a paper. The dream-quality of her reflections are related to the horror of a world of action in which suffering, decisions, personalities, are immediately revealed.

The technical difference between *The Mark on the Wall* and *Kew Gardens* is that in the first, consciousness is centred in her own mind ; in the second it is diffused among different centres. The garden itself is now the channel for thought. It is no longer a question of thoughts passing through her mind, but of light, insects, people, sounds, passing through the garden. The dimensions of the objects seen do not remain at the steady human size to which novelists have accustomed us ; they suddenly diminish to the consciousness of a snail, who sees cliffs and lakes and round boulders of grey stone between the passage from one stalk to another ; then suddenly they swing to the vast bird's-eye view from an aeroplane flying above the trees. " Yellow and black, pink and snow-white, shapes of all these colours, men, women and children were spotted for a second upon the horizon. and then, seeing the breadth of yellow that lay upon the grass, they wavered and sought shade beneath the trees, dissolving like drops of water in the yellow and green atmosphere, staining it faintly with red and blue."

To let the perspective shift from high to low, from huge to microscopic, to let figures of people, insects, aeroplanes, flowers pass across the vision and melt away—these are devices common enough to another form of art. They are the tricks of the cinema. Mrs. Woolf had discovered the cinema. There is no reason why it should monopolise powers of expansion and contraction. In *Kew Gardens* the external figures appear and disappear with such brilliant clarity that we could almost photograph them from the words. It becomes plain at once that here is a technique of writing which a novelist could use, given a keen visual imagination and a strong sense of design.

But external forms are not everything. Could the same free technique be applied to the fragments of thought, sounds heard, pictures seen, passing through the mind ? When one sits in front of a fire, the thoughts are not always so fully formed as in *The Mark on the Wall*. Dare one photograph by a mental camera the far more elusive procession of fancy, conversation, memory, reflection, of which one is conscious while, say, pouring out tea on a foggy afternoon ?

Mrs. Woolf's attempt to do this, she calls *Monday or Tuesday*. It is very brief, and is, perhaps, the most obscure of all her sketches. Possibly she chose it to give the title to her collection because it is the high-water mark of experiment. Further than this she dared not go. Beyond this point of individualism art ceases to be communicative ; it becomes pure expression—an activity which may gratify the artist, but which has no more social significance than an exercise performed by a dancer in her private bathroom.

" Lazy and indifferent, shaking space easily from his wings, knowing his way, the heron passes over the church beneath the sky. White and distant, absorbed in itself, endlessly the sky covers and uncovers, moves and remains. A lake ? Blot the shores of it out ! A mountain ? Oh, perfect—the sun gold on its slopes. Down that falls. Ferns then, or white feathers, for ever and ever.

" Desiring truth, awaiting it, laboriously distilling a few words, for ever desiring—(a cry starts to the left, another to the right. Wheels strike divergently. Omnibuses conglomerate in conflict)—for ever desiring—(the clock asseverates with twelve distinct strokes that it is mid-day ; light sheds gold scales ; children swarm)—for ever desiring truth. Red is the dome ; coins hang on the trees ; smoke trails from the chimney ; bark, shout, cry ' Iron for sale '—and truth ?

" Radiating to a point men's feet and women's feet,

black or gold encrusted—(this foggy weather—Sugar ?
No, thank you—The commonwealth of the future)—
the firelight darting and making the room red, save
for the black figures and their bright eyes, while outside a van discharges, Miss Thingummy drinks tea at
her desk, and plate-glass preserves fur coats——"

It begins, apparently, with a mental picture. The
mind sees a bird—a heron. The bird symbol is a
favourite one. Mrs. Dalloway is like a blue jay ;
happiness is identified in *Orlando* with a kingfisher or
heron's feather, ecstasy with a wild goose ; in *An
Unwritten Novel* the artist becomes " the hawk over
the down." In *Jacob's Room* the metaphor reappears.
The heron flies over an imagined landscape.

But while the visual imagination forms pictures, the
will is at work, desiring that which Mrs. Woolf's will
always desires—truth, the means to capture truth, to
distil it in a few words. Then, breaking in upon will
and imagination come the sounds from the street, with
their impact upon the alert and waiting senses.
Imagination, will, fancy, registration by the senses of
external experience, combine together in " Red is the
dome ; coins hang on the trees ; smoke trails from the
chimneys ; bark, shout, cry ' Iron for sale '—and
truth ? " But we must have action as well. One
cannot sit by a fireside registering sensations. Someone comes in for coffee after lunch—or possibly tea.
The room by this time is dark enough to show the
firelight, and outside in the town Miss Thingummy
—all-the-Secretaries-in-the-world—drinks tea at her
desk. One must permit conversation, on the foggy

weather, on the Commonwealth of the Future, and make polite inquiries about sugar.

This is more than cinematograph technique. It is like an orchestra. Senses, thoughts, emotions, will, memory, fancies, the impact of the outside world, action and conversation each play a different instrument. Mrs. Woolf is now a conductor. She raises her arms, beckoning now to fancy, now to power, now to a noise of traffic from the street, now a polite inquiry about sugar. It is immensely complicated, immensely suggestive. The whole orchestra gets going at once, responsive to her beat. She must keep control. She must make some sort of harmony, of melody, some intelligible rhythm, some sequence that the listener can follow, or the music will dissolve into a confused cacophony of sound.

The question is, Can she do it ? And the answer seems to be that it can be done, but only with extreme care, and only after most careful preparation of the audience. In *Jacob's Room* she uses the cinematograph method. In *Mrs. Dalloway* and *To the Lighthouse* she conducts the orchestra.

So she had got free. The old clumsy tools were out of the window. She had learned to use new and far more delicate and complex instruments. Writing had ceased to be a discipline and had become an adventure. It was true that her experience of life was still limited. She could not rattle round St. Petersburg, rape peasant girls, fight in the Crimea, manage estates, and lay up an enormous store of memories of action. Tolstoi's advantages were as far remote from her as ever. But she had something. If her knowledge of life was narrow, it was profound. There was no fear, no sorrow, no ecstasy, and no limitation that she could not penetrate. And now she had an entirely new technique. She could compensate herself for all the things she did not know by arranging in a thousand new patterns the things she did.

And suddenly, it seemed, something happened to her spirits. She learned gaiety. The little sketch called *A Society* is on an entirely new note. There had been comedy in *The Voyage Out* and humour in *Night and Day*, but in neither novel had there been gaiety. Now, in this strange little squib, gaiety dances ; it is evanescent with hyperbole ; it is debonair with nonsense. The mood was to reappear in *Orlando* ; it was to lurk in fragments of *A Room of One's Own*. It is almost as though directly Mrs. Woolf abandoned comedy she discovered laughter.

She did not use it for long ; her sense of life is tragic rather than comic. But having discovered it, she never lost it again. Perhaps laughter is the first gift of freedom. In any case, after the publication of *Monday or Tuesday*, any discerning reader must have understood that Mrs. Woolf was free.

VI
CINEMATOGRAPH

IN 1922, the year following *Monday or Tuesday*, Mrs. Woolf published *Jacob's Room*. It is her war book. It is as much a war book as *The Death of a Hero* or *Farewell to Arms*; yet it never mentions trenches, camps, recruiting officers, nor latrines. It does not describe the hero's feelings on the eve of battle; not an inch of barbed wire decorates its foreground. These things, of course, are relevant to modern war, but Mrs. Woolf does not describe them. She knew, perhaps, that her talent is unsuited to the description of violence in action, though she can measure with extraordinary range and accuracy its effect when action has ceased.

She lacks the particular type of imagination which enables Naomi Mitchison, for instance, to enter so freely the consciousness of her combative barbarians. She could not know in what terms Tommies referred to their sergeant-major nor what it feels like to thrust a bayonet through a belly. What she did know, what she could imagine, was what life looked like to those young men who in 1914 and 1915 crossed the Channel and vanished out of English life for ever. When such a young man was killed, she seems to ask, what was lost then? What lost by him? What was lost by his friends? What exactly was it that had disappeared?

In *Jacob's Room* she answers, " It was this."

The theme of the novel is the same as that of *The Voyage Out*. It is the masculine counterpart of that feminine story. Rachel Vinrace was educated for a life which led to premature death in South America ; Jacob Flanders was educated for life which led to premature death in battle. The theme of the two books is identical ; but their treatment is altogether different. In *Jacob's Room* Mrs. Woolf built for the first time a complete novel with her new tools, and chose for it the cinematograph technique tried out in *Kew Gardens*. Almost any page in the book could be transferred straight on to a film. The story deals mainly with the external evidence of emotions, even thoughts and memories assuming pictorial quality. Sometimes, it is true, the action passes to that confused twilight which dwells within the mind ; but for the most part it is indicated by the changing positions and gestures of the characters. Betty Flanders weeps, strokes the cat Topaz, writes letters ; Jacob yawns, stretches, reads ; Florinda draws her cloak about her to hide the evidence of her pregnancy. It is a picture-maker's novel.

It is not a perfectly easy book to read. Its obscurity puzzled a good many intelligent people when it was published, for Mrs. Woolf gives no clue to her intention. There is no preliminary announcement, as on a film, " Produced by —— Scenario by —— From the story of ——" But the first chapter betrays her method. Its scenario might be summarised, " Jacob as a small boy at the seaside in Cornwall," and Mrs. Woolf begins, as any producer might, by photographing a letter, word by word welling out slowly from the gold nib of Betty Flanders' pen. " So of course there was nothing for it but to leave." She shows us next the complete figure of the woman pressing her heels deeper in the sand to give her matronly body a firmer seat ; then there is a close-up of her face, maternal, tearful, because Scarborough, where Captain Barfoot is, seems so far from Cornwall where she sits writing. The camera swings round then to photograph the entire bay, yacht and lighthouse, quivering through her tears, and flashes back to indicate a blot spreading across the writing paper.

There are two little boys, Archer and Jacob ; but Archer cannot find Jacob, who has a habit of wandering off by himself, and Betty Flanders' mind—and the film—return to the situation which caused the tears to flow, Seabrook Flanders' death. Betty Flanders has been a widow for two years. She lives in Scarborough with her sons, and the rector's wife thinks in church, looking at her when the organ plays, that " marriage is a fortress and widows stray solitary in the open fields, picking up stones, gleaning a few golden straws, lonely, unprotected, poor creatures."

Ferreting in her bag for a stamp, rising to go, Betty Flanders disturbs the painter, Charles Steele, who was using her figure to balance the colours of his landscape. Archer runs across, shouting " Ja-cob ! Ja-cob ! " and Mrs. Flanders picks up her parasol.

But Jacob is off by himself, climbing a rock, teasing a crab, running away from a couple of trippers stretched on the sand, and comforting himself for the desolation of being alone, by the sight of a skull, "perhaps a cow's skull, a skull perhaps, with the teeth in it," lying under the cliff.

The picture moves on, showing Betty Flanders leading her children back to their lodgings, forgetting the meat, and greeting the maid, Rebecca. It shows the bare sitting-room of the lodgings by lamplight, the light streaming through the window into the wet garden, lighting up a child's bucket and a purple aster drenched in the rain. It shows the children in bed, Archer wakeful, Jacob asleep with the sheep's jawbone at his feet. Mrs. Flanders soothes Archer frightened by the storm by telling him that the steamer won't sink. " ' The Captain's in bed long ago. Shut your eyes, and think of the fairies, fast asleep, under the flowers.' " The details of that composition are to be used again in *To the Lighthouse*—the bare, sea-surrounded bedroom, the children in bed, the skull, and Mrs. Ramsay soothing the wakeful Cam, telling her how lovely the skull looks now with her shawl draped round it ; " how the fairies would love it ; it was like a bird's nest ; it was like a beautiful mountain such as she had seen abroad, with valleys and flowers and bells ringing and birds singing and little goats and antelopes. . . ." There is a dream-like quality about it, as of a memory from early childhood, impressed upon the mind of a sensitive, nervous child by an understanding mother. It tranquillises the picture, befitting the external vision of Mrs. Flanders and Rebecca bending over the cot of the smallest child, " conspirators plotting the eternal conspiracy of hush and clean bottles."

The section closes with a return to the rain-washed garden, and the crab caught by Jacob, vainly trying to escape from its bucket-prison, " trying again and falling back, and trying again and again."

The combination of elements here is masterly—Betty Flanders' care for her children, and her helplessness ; Jacob's running off alone so that Archer must call after him, " ' Ja-cob ! Ja-cob ! ' " his voice having " an extraordinary sadness. Pure from all body, pure from all passion, going out unto the world, solitary, unanswered, breaking against rocks—so it sounded." So, all through the book, Betty Flanders is to care for her children—and be impotent ; so Jacob is to go off adventuring alone, till he adventures out of life altogether at the end ; so, in his empty rooms, in the last chapter, his friend Bonamy is to call, " ' Jacob ! Jacob ! ' " and no Jacob will answer. Only Mrs. Flanders, bursting open the bedroom door, holds up a pair of Jacob's shoes and asks, " ' What am I to do with these, Mr. Bonamy ? ' " and to that question there is, indeed, no satisfactory answer. The picture seems to compose a sort of refrain to the novel. It leaves an impression of apprehension, of the solicitude of women and of the indifference of fate which abandons opal-shelled crabs to the mercilessness of children, and abandons children to the mercilessness of war. Its melancholy, its extraordinary desolation, are indefinable.

The next chapter shows both Mrs. Woolf and her

method at their worst. The scene is laid in Scarborough. The people are Betty Flanders and her neighbours ; Captain Barfoot, an almost purely " literary " figure ; a vague Rector's wife ; a love-sick curate. Jacob himself, a schoolboy, collecting butterflies, is less definite here than elsewhere. Mrs. Woolf is clearly not at home in this provincial bourgeois household. Nobody comes to life.

One stroke in her portrait of Betty Flanders, however, is noteworthy, and that is the incident of Mr. Floyd, the curate, who proposed to her, and whom she did not like, because he had red hair. When he leaves for a parish in Sheffield, being unable to endure Scarborough, one imagines, after his rejection, he gives John Flanders a kitten ; and years afterwards, when Betty reads in the *Scarborough and Harrogate Courier* that the Rev. Andrew Floyd has been made Principal of Maresfield House, she gets up and goes over to the fender and strokes the cat, whose fur was the colour of Mr. Floyd's hair.

" ' Poor old Topaz,' said Mrs. Flanders, as he stretched himself out in the sun, and she smiled, thinking how she had had him gelded, and how she did not like red hair in men. Smiling, she went into the kitchen."

Now that, with its delicately suggested hint of cruelty and coarseness in a good and simple woman, has shocked many of Mrs. Woolf's admirers. But it is true. Good women frequently would be shocked to recognise their own motives. Betty Flanders quite probably would have derived satisfaction from her

vicarious gelding of Mr. Floyd. As the episode
stands, it gives a queer flavour of pungency to a picture
which might otherwise have been too smooth and
sweet.

There is one other interesting passage in the chapter,
revealing that inter-relationship of all Mrs. Woolf's
novels which gives the impressive sense of unity to her
work. Seabrook Flanders is dead. His widow has
put on his tombstone " Merchant of this City " to
impress the boys rather than to record a truth, for
Seabrook had been in life a rolling stone, and only sat
for three months behind an office window. But Betty,
looking at the grave, wonders what he had been.
" Had he then been nothing ? An unanswerable
question, since even if it weren't the habit of the under-
taker to close the eyes, the light so soon goes out of
them. At first, part of herself, now one of a company,
he had merged in the grass, the sloping hillside, the
thousand white stones, some slanting, others upright,
the decayed wreaths, the crosses of green tin, the narrow
yellow paths . . . Seabrook was now all that ; and
when, with her skirt hitched up, feeding the chickens,
she heard the bell for service or funeral, that was
Seabrook's voice—the voice of the dead." What is
it ? What is it ? Her mind reiterates. What happens
to the dead ? For what is life ? Is Seabrook now like
Wordsworth's Lucy—

> " No motion has she now, no force ;
>   She neither hears nor sees ;
> Rolled round in earth's diurnal course
>   With rocks and stones and trees " ?

Is he like Virginia Woolf's Mrs. Ramsay in *To the Lighthouse*? Who, after she was dead, still left her shawl hanging from the skull in the children's bedroom, protective even in death, till it loosened itself, corner by corner, " with a roar, with a rupture, as after centuries of quiescence a rock rends itself from the mountain and hurtles crashing into the valley." Mrs. Ramsay is dead, rolled round with rocks and stones and trees. Her shawl, so soft, so protective, yet becomes part of that unity, that impersonal universe. Like a rock it falls. It crashes into the valley. In and in works the unifying mind, seeking, as Keats sought in his metaphors, as Shakespeare sought, as Wordsworth sought, some binding unity, some permanent and satisfying relationship between life and death and rocks and people.

If the Scarborough chapter is, apart from its relationship to Mrs. Woolf's ideas of life and death, a little dull and obscure, the Cambridge chapter is pure magic. Cambridge glows with all the romantic glamour with which her imagination might have invested it had she seen it first when she was young and impressionable, and had spent a wonderful May Week with her brothers. The method employed is still the method of the cinema.

Picture follows picture, each one touched with an almost unearthly glamour. The train to Cambridge, a service at King's College, the comic lunch with a don, the river, the quadrangle—they are entrancing. It is true that though Mrs. Woolf might be in love with Cambridge, she was not overmuch impressed by its high-priests. " It is not simple or pure, or wholly splendid, the lamp of learning," she informs us. The old men, whose heads are so full of knowledge, are, as often as not, twisted and queer as cactuses. Huxtable cannot walk straight after his port. Sopwith praises the sky, night after night, for twenty years. Cowan chuckles at the same stories. Learning can sometimes be, Mrs. Woolf insists, at odds with art. Learning can sometimes degenerate into superstition. Learning by no means always makes for wisdom. One is reminded of that passage in *The Mark on the Wall* when she reflects how admirable the world might be without specialists or learned men. She is affected too, partly perhaps, by the prohibitions which she describes in *A Room of One's Own*—prohibitions which order women out of libraries and off the grass. Yet her pictures of the dons themselves—Sopwith, Huxtable and Cowan—are admirably done, with justice and understanding as well as humour—especially the picture of Sopwith, to whom a man could say anything, who sat in his room, cutting cake, talking to undergraduates.

Mrs. Woolf can be just even where she has no particular liking ; but where she likes, her pictures become radiant. The May air of the Cambridge spring, when Jacob escapes from the luncheon party and sculls up the river with Tim Durrant ; Neville's Court by night, the window-boxes foaming with flowers, the window lit ; Jacob's room, with its round table, low chairs, yellow flags in a jar on the mantelpiece, his essay manuscript, his notes, his pipes—these are pure poetry. The young men meet and argue about Keats. Jacob comes to the window. "He looked satisfied ; indeed masterly, which expression changed slightly as he stood there ; the sound of the clock conveying to him (it may be) a sense of old buildings and time ; and himself the inheritor ; and then to-morrow ; and friends ; at the thought of whom, in sheer confidence and pleasure, it seemed, he yawned and stretched himself." We are reminded, by this tragic confidence, of Rachel and Terence, who were equally assured of life, equally doomed. " ' Well, Rachel,' " Terence said, after drawing a picture of their future life together in London, " ' we shall be doing that together in six weeks' time, and it'll be the middle of June then,—and June in London—my God ! How pleasant it all is ! '

" ' And we're certain to have it too,' she said. ' It isn't as if we were expecting a great deal—only to walk about and look at things.' "

" Certain to have it ? " With death always imminent ? Jacob was certain. The others left him alone with a man called Simeon, talking about Julian the Apostate. The room was full of intimacy, still, deep, like a pool.

" But Jacob moved. He murmured good-night. He went out into the court. He buttoned his jacket across his chest. He went back to his rooms, and being the only man who walked at the moment back to his rooms, his footsteps rang out. His figure loomed large. Back from the Chapel, back from the Hall, back from the Library, came the sound of his footsteps, as if the old stone echoed with magisterial authority. The young man—the young man—the young man—back to his rooms."

Now that is prose which uses every device of poetry save unbroken rhythm. It has rhythm, but it would not be as easy to arrange in *vers libre* as *A Haunted House*. The cadences are musical, but they are the music of prose. Sound and sense are allied. The plangent reiteration echoes the sound of footsteps. Mrs. Woolf has reached a combination of poetic and cinema technique which is almost wholly satisfying.

Chapter IV concerns the boating holiday when Jacob and Timmy Durrant go to Cornwall by way of the Scilly Isles. The first picture is a sea piece with the delicate sunlit colours of Russell Flint. The young men quarrel and enjoy themselves. There follows one of Mrs. Woolf's characteristic devices, a picture of the mainland from the sea.

" The mainland, not so very far off—you could see clefts in the cliffs, white cottages, smoke going up— wore an extraordinary look of calm, of sunny peace, as if wisdom and piety had descended upon the dwellers there. Now a cry sounded as of a man calling pilchards in a main street. It wore an extraordinary look of piety and peace, as if old men smoked by the door, and girls stood, hands on hips, at the well, and horses stood ; as if the end of the world had come, and cabbage fields and stone walls and coastguard stations, and above all, the white sand bays with the waves breaking unseen by anyone, rose to heaven in a kind of ecstasy.

" But imperceptibly the cottage smoke droops, has the look of a mourning emblem, a flag floating its caress over a grave. The gulls, making their broad flight and then riding at peace, seem to mark the grave.

" No doubt if this were Italy, Greece, or even the shores of Spain, sadness would be routed by strangeness and excitement and the nudge of a classical education. But the Cornish hills have stark chimneys standing on them ; and, somehow or other, loveliness is infernally sad. Yes, the chimneys and the coast-guard stations and the little bays with the waves breaking unseen by anyone make all remember the overpowering sorrow. And what can this sorrow be ?

" It is brewed by the earth itself. It comes from the houses on the coast. We start transparent, then the cloud thickens. All history backs our pane of glass. To escape is vain."

Now that passage says a great many things. It gives a pictorial description of the Cornish coast. It hints by colloquial phrases, " loveliness is infernally sad," that the picture is seen by the young men from the boat. It hints by a remote reference to Shelley— " All history backs our pane of glass."—" A dome of many-coloured glass " ?—that they are literary young men. It conveys an impression of melancholy which is a common enough experience to persons of sensibility who look at land from the detachment of the water, and it ends with a characteristic gesture of debonair uncertainty :

" But whether this is the right interpretation of

Jacob's gloom as he sat naked, in the sun, looking at Land's End, it is impossible to say ; for he never spoke a word."

The holiday continues. Mrs. Durrant, Tim's mother, one of those old iron aristocrats admired by Mrs. Woolf, patronises the cottager, Mrs. Pascoe ; Jacob and Tim join the house party ; there is a dinner ; there are girls on the terrace, in the drawing-room, in yellow and blue and silver gauze, like a Whistler picture ; Clara Durrant—a Meredithian heroine—cuts grapes high on a ladder for Jacob to take back with him, and gives her heart as well. We are left uncertain of his condition. There are obscurities here. There is a joke about begonias which, after prolonged contemplation, I am quite unable to fathom. But by this time the style is growing easier.

Next, there is Jacob, settled in an eighteenth-century house in Bloomsbury, going daily to an office, having acquired a friend with a Wellington nose called Bonamy. It is a rather sober and sombre picture, full of buses and clerks and a blind beggar woman in the London streets. Then Jacob becomes Bohemian, and at a Guy Fawkes party on Parliament Hill ?—somewhere certainly where the light from a bonfire can show St. Paul's—he meets Florinda, who is a young woman not at all of the type familiar to Clara Durrant, a young woman who lives a life of a doubtful virtue, in a cheap mustard-coloured bedroom, half attic, half studio.

The Florinda chapters, with their irony and understanding, are magnificent. They treat, of course, of sex. Florinda was, though in a Chelseaesque and amateurish way, a prostitute ; she " caught " the innocent Jacob, ready game for even so casual a huntress. But Mrs. Woolf is not shocked. She is not solemn. She can, it appears, regard sex with steady and amused comprehension. Florinda said she was a virgin, which was doubtful. " But whether or not she was a virgin seems a matter of no importance whatever," says Mrs. Woolf, " unless, indeed, it is the only thing of any importance at all." Then, ironically, she draws her picture of the London streets, with men and women seething up and down the well-worn beats. " Late homecomers could see shadows against the blinds even in the most respectable suburbs. Not a square in snow or fog lacked its amorous couple. All plays turned on the same subject ; yet we say it is a matter of no importance at all.

" If Florinda had a mind, she might have read with clearer eyes than we can. She and her sort have solved the question by turning it into a trifle of washing the hands nightly before going to bed, the only difficulty being whether you prefer your water hot or cold, which being settled, the mind can go about its business unassailed."

Now that, for a woman writing in 1922, was an unexpected attitude. It was the attitude of one who dared to regard sex with the same unalarmed detachment with which she regarded the coast of Cornwall. And with humour. Whatever the other Georgians thought about sex, they regarded it with solemnity. The disciples of D. H. Lawrence, James Joyce or

Middleton Murry might smile at religion, and shrug their shoulders at sociology. But Sex is serious. It is as though they could never follow Mrs. Woolf's habit of pushing off in a boat from the mainland and regarding it dispassionately with detachment from the sea.

But Mrs. Woolf can. Even when Jacob finds that Florinda is faithless, and his disappointment turns London into a nightmare of squalor wherein the nightingales themselves are obscene, even then Mrs. Woolf remains objective, interested, a trifle amused. She employs her old trick of drawing all the external world, the streets and the lights and the voices, and a picture of the winter's night, bitterly cold in the frost outside, into her conspiracy to show how Jacob felt about Florinda. But she knew also that such feelings do not endure for long in healthy young men like Jacob Flanders.

He is a healthy young man. Though his conduct with Florinda is not at all of the kind likely to reassure his mother in Scarborough, writing letters with her toes on the fender, and hoping that all is well with the boy, it does not damage him. For when he emerges from his bedroom door, followed by Florinda yawning and arranging her hair, he comes " in his dressing-gown, amiable, authoritative, beautifully healthy like a baby after an airing, with an eye as clear as running water." As a necessary, interesting, but not overwhelmingly important episode in life, Mrs. Woolf puts sex in its place.

The whole Florinda episode is set into the proportion which Mrs. Woolf thinks fitting for it, partly by its companion picture of Clara Durrant's life, and partly by the first hint of coming catastrophe, which will blow to pieces this carefully constructed world.

While Jacob is consorting with Florinda, and later with Laurette and Fanny and Sandra Wentworth Williams, Clara Durrant, who loves him, leads the life of a debutante. She buys carnations ; she attends the dressmaker ; she introduces guests at her mother's parties ; she practises a little mild philanthropy to the poor of Notting Hill and Clerkenwell. The same routine of social obligation which had bound Katharine Hilbery binds her. It frustrates her opportunity of knowing Jacob as it frustrates her opportunity of learning Italian or playing on the piano more than one sonata. Clara has not Katharine Hilbery's force of intellect or character, nor the raw intelligence of Rachel Vinrace, but she sometimes surprises observers by a strength of emotion which suggests something almost heroic in her character.

All this, however, is subordinated to the dress-makers and parties. Without a word of theorising or protest, Mrs. Woolf suggests the contrast between the lives of young men and young women in pre-war society. Jacob is so firm, so reticent, romantic, adventurous, passing from adventures of education to adventures of sex, and from these to adventures of travel and work and danger. Clara is so vague and shadowy and blushing, bending her pretty head over paper flowers, leaving calling-cards, driving to the Opera, weeping after proposals, a creature of hesitations, emotions, acquiescences, her only strength in love, and that doomed to frustration. Bonamy, Jacob's friend, could not help feeling compassion for her, even while he marvelled at the insipidity of an "existence squeezed and emasculated within a white satin shoe."

That is one contrast. If Jacob knows disillusionment and ugliness, Clara never has any chance of knowing anything more than wishes unfulfilled. The pictures in which she appears are drawn always in the same soft, rosy colours, whereas Jacob's spin from violence of vivid light to darkness. It is Clara for whom one feels compassion, even after Jacob's moment of anguish in Soho, knowing that Florinda is false to him.

But contrasted with the picture from Clara's life is the foreboding of Jacob's coming death. Right in the middle of the Florinda episode Mrs. Woolf hints it. She shows us Rose Shaw talking to Mr. Bowley about a certain Jimmy who refused to marry a girl called Helen Aitken. . . . "And now Jimmy feeds crows in Flanders and Helen visits hospitals. Oh, life is damnable, life is wicked, as Rose Shaw said." That is all. A little, apparently irrelevant interpolation, a flash forward across some years ; for this all takes place before the war. Yet it has been set there deliberately, perhaps to show us that life's anguish is made tolerable only when balanced by death.

Life may be wicked, but it is better than non-existence ; it is better than Clara Durrant's half-life. The pictures continue. They increase in brilliance and variety. Jacob recovers from Florinda, lunches with a countess, hunts in Essex, argues with Bonamy, takes tea with ladies, reads in the British Museum, goes to a party in Hammersmith and walks home afterwards feeling that life is good. He spends a reasonable evening with a prostitute called Laurette, and flutters the heart of an artist's model, Fanny Elmer. He goes to Paris, and finds that city and the people who live there more wonderful than anything in the world, for, in spite of his looks, his solidity and his reticence, he is still very young and naïve. He visits Italy ; he visits Athens ; he falls in love with an experienced married woman travelling with her bored politician husband ; he accompanies them to Constantinople. He returns to London in the height of the season, his pockets full of Greek notes, giving no thought to Clara, Fanny or Florinda, though all three thought of him. Florinda was going to have a baby by Nick Bramham. The question of her virginity, then, was settled, and in the way least comfortable to herself. Sandra Wentworth Williams looked at her own little boy, and decided that Jacob, for all his good looks and solidity, was a small boy himself. But all the time, as Jacob sat in the Park, as Clara drove to the opera, as Florinda bargained with Nick Bramham in Verrey's, and Betty Flanders wrote her letters, the war was closing down on them.

Very quietly Mrs. Woolf conveys the impression of war, like fate, closing down upon her characters. There is first that hint of Jimmy killed and Helen visiting hospitals—no word of explanation why this

should have happened. Nearly a hundred pages
further on, as Mrs. Bowley is handing strawberries
in the Durrants' drawing-room, we are told, " The
battleships ray out over the North Sea." Old General
Gibbon asks, " Where are the men ? . . . Where are
the guns ? " When Jacob returns from Greece, and
sits in Hyde Park thinking of Sandra's letters, Clara,
doomed to miss him, exercises her terrier and, with
half her mind on Jacob, worries with the other half
about her mother, who is much disturbed by the
position of England. Mr. Bowley reassures her,
" England's all right." But meanwhile a procession
with banners passes down Whitehall. At the
Admiralty news is received of the Reichstag. Clerks
transmit rumours from Vienna ; their faces grow
grave as they write ; Timmy Durrant is among the
clerks. The Cabinet meets. " Sixteen gentlemen
lifting their pens or turning perhaps wearily in their
chairs, decreed that the course of history should
shape itself this way." A placard is tied round a
lamp-post in Whitehall. " ' The Kaiser,' a far-away
voice remarks, " ' received me in audience.' " Out in
Greece, where Jacob has been so recently, " the ships
in the Piræus fired their guns. The sound spread
itself flat, and then went tunnelling its way with fitful
explosions among the channels of the islands. Darkness drops like a knife over Greece."

" ' The guns ? ' said Betty Flanders half asleep,
getting out of bed and going to the window, which
was decorated with a fringe of dark leaves. ' Not at
this distance,' she thought. ' It is the sea.' Again,

far away, she heard the dull sound, as if nocturnal women were beating great carpets. There was Morty lost, and Seabrook dead ; her sons fighting for their Country. But were the chickens safe ? Was that someone moving downstairs ? Rebecca with the toothache ? No. The nocturnal women were beating great carpets. Her hens shifted slightly on their perches."

There is only one more picture. Betty Flanders and Bonamy go to tidy up Jacob's room. " ' He left everything just as it was,' Bonamy marvelled. . . . ' What did he expect ? Did he think he would come back ? ' "

It is clear that he will not come back. He has gone for ever. His room, his bills, his letters, his invitations are all that remain, and his old shoes in the bedroom. The survivors must dispose somehow of these possessions, more durable than their owner. Jacob's room is empty, save for these. All the world has, indeed, been Jacob's room—Cornwall, Scarborough, London, Italy, Athens. Nothing remains now except what he has discarded. What has been lost ? These have been lost to Jacob ; Jacob has been lost to Bonamy and to his mother, to Clara and Fanny and Sandra. The possession and the loss are double. We dwell in ourselves ; we dwell in the mirror that lies in the eyes of our friends regarding us. This, it would seem, is what this novel means.

As an accomplishment, it was something of a *tour de force*. It took literary England by storm. Here was something new, strange, beautiful. " It is authentic poetry, cognisant of the soul," said Rebecca West. " It is a novel in a thousand," said several others. It was, indeed, a triumphant experiment in a new technique.

But now that we can set it beside Mrs. Woolf's later work, beside *Mrs. Dalloway* and *To the Lighthouse* and *The Waves*, we know that it was not the best that she could do. The cinematograph style was brilliantly effective, but it was not as subtle as the orchestral effect which she was to use in *To the Lighthouse* ; she was to obtain a surer control over her material in *Mrs. Dalloway*. She was to adventure further into obscure realms of human consciousness in *The Waves*. The contrasts, perhaps, in *Jacob's Room* are too violent. There are obscurities which even the most diligent study cannot penetrate. The effect created is very largely visual. Later she would plunge into the nerves, the brain, the senses of her characters, exploring further, yet binding the whole more closely into a unity of mood.

As for her sense of life, it shines vividly through every page, varied, exquisite, but not insipid. There runs, indeed, all through *Jacob's Room* a hint of cruelty : the crab tries to escape from the bucket ; kind Mrs. Flanders smiles at Topaz ; Jacob neglects Clara ; Florinda has a baby by the wrong man ; Sandra Wentworth Williams is heartless ; Jacob dies.

The world, with all its beauty and adventure, its richness and variety, is darkened by cruelty. Death, if it ends the loveliness, the adventure, ends also that. Death balances the picture. It completes the pattern. It makes even cruelty fall into place. It is completion.

VII
THE ADVENTURE JUSTIFIED

I SUPPOSE that if *Jacob's Room* had fallen as flat as the first publication of *Du Côté de chez Swann*, Mrs. Woolf would still have continued to experiment ; but its success must have influenced her a little. To an artist of her type communication and intelligibility are not negligible. The novel form is, after all, only a kind of shorthand by which the reader is given to understand much more than the writer sets down. Unless we are familiar with the convention, we may make no more of the meaning than a horse makes of an etching of a carrot. A sudden change in the code may cut off all communication between writer and reader.

In *Jacob's Room*, Mrs. Woolf had taken great liberties with the conventions.

She had thrown overboard much that had been commonly considered indispensable to the novel : descriptions of places and families, explanations of environment, a plot of external action, dramatic scenes, climaxes, conclusions, and almost all those link-sentences which bind one episode to the next. But much remained to her. She had retained her preoccupation with life and death, with character, and with the effect of characters grouped and inter-acting. She had kept her consciousness of time and movement. She knew how present and past are interwoven, and how to-day depends so much upon knowledge and memory of yesterday, and fear for or confidence in to-morrow. She was still preoccupied with moral values ; she was immensely excited about form and the way in which the patterns of life grow more and more complex as one regards them. And she was more sure now both of herself and of her public. She dared take greater risks with them, confident that they would not let her down.

In the two novels which immediately followed *Jacob's Room*—*Mrs. Dalloway* and *To the Lighthouse*—Mrs. Woolf developed still further the experimental methods which she had tried out in *Monday or Tuesday*. In them, form and substance were even more closely related. And again her consciousness of time played a substantial part in the experiment.

In each of the three books, however, she assumes a different attitude towards time. In *Jacob's Room*, the events follow each other, for the most part, in chronological sequence. Sometimes she chooses to show us two or three incidents happening simultaneously : Florinda sick, and Clara asleep on her pillow ; or Mrs. Pascoe watching the steamers off the Cornish coast, and the red light on the Parthenon ; or Jacob looking at his butterflies, and his memories of how he caught them.

In *Mrs. Dalloway* she leads us a step further. The external action of *Jacob's Room* covered some twenty odd years. In *Mrs. Dalloway* it covers little more than twelve hours, from the morning when Mrs. Dalloway decides that she will buy her own flowers for the party that evening, till the climax of the party when, having said good-bye to the Prime Minister and having returned from her brief withdrawal into the little room, she approaches her old suitor, Peter Walsh. But within that cup, that little enclosed bowl of time, the waters of the past and future rock and swirl ; the past, far back to Clarissa's childhood at Bourton, the future, forward to a time when she would not exist, save as part of the trees and flowers and sunshine that she so much loved. Each moment becomes enriched by other moments ; consciousness is never simple.

In *To the Lighthouse* she faces time afresh. It is not only the impersonal moment which draws all past and present to itself, it is a person. First Mrs. Ramsay, then Lily Briscoe draw all time, all life, all movement into themselves. In *Mrs. Dalloway* incidents spread themselves out through different human perceptions : a car drives up Bond Street ; it is heard by Mrs. Dalloway, by Miss Pym selling flowers, by Edgar J. Watkiss with his roll of piping, by Septimus Warren Smith, by Sir John Buckhurst, by Moll Pratt, by strangers looking in hat-shop windows who instantly think of the dead, of the flag, of Empire ; by a Colonial, who insults the House of Windsor, and by the crowd gathered round the gates of Buckingham Palace ; out and out spread the ripples from the stone dropped into the pool that is London on a June morning. But in *To the Lighthouse* Mrs. Ramsay sits in a window, and into her mind come thoughts of her little boy James, of her husband, her daughters, of Charles Tansley and Lily Briscoe, and of all the practical reforms, the necessity for which she can see so clearly—the need for a clean milk supply, better housing for the poor, something to be done about cancer. In and in they press upon her mind, filling it, bearing her down with their burden ; the hour, the moment, being filled to full measure, pressed down, shaken together, and running over.

To write of time in these different guises, different forms are needed. For *Jacob's Room* the cinematograph form sufficed. Picture can follow picture when the chronology is comparatively straightforward ; but *Mrs. Dalloway* demanded the more subtle complexity of orchestration. Into those hours of one London day are enclosed beauty and horror, gaiety and madness, jealousy stirring like a snake under the flowers, all time past remembered by each of the characters, so that no page can be opened without finding the whole orchestra in full swing—mind, senses, the memory, external action, reference, like so many instruments, flutes, violins, drums, trumpets, playing together. Peter Walsh sits in the park and thinks of Clarissa. He begins by leaping to false conclusions about Septimus and Lucrezia Warren Smith ; he goes on to think of youth generally ; of the fun of returning to England ; of London parks ; of his own susceptibility to impressions ; of changes in women between 1918 and 1923 ; of Sally Seton ; of all Clarissa's friends ; of Hugh Whitbread ; of a Sunday morning at Bourton when Sally Seton lashed out about women's rights ; of Mrs. Hugh Whitbread ; of his, Peter's, own plight, being out of a job at fifty-three ; of Richard

Dalloway ; of how Richard had dealt with Clarissa's dog ; of how he was a bore and a prig ; of Sally again, and her agreement with Peter about Clarissa's marriage ; . . . on and on it goes, the free-association method of *The Mark on the Wall* enriched by the orchestration of *Monday or Tuesday*, the whole gathered into its perfect bowl of external time, and given a unity not only of form—all closed in on itself, without even chapter-divisions—but of tone ; even the horror and violence of the suicide somehow softened and brought into relationship with Clarissa's party, as though the discipline which surrounds a lady of fashion were adequate to subdue death and distraction themselves to the silvery elegance of a drawing-room in June.

To the Lighthouse is much less concentrated. The book is in two halves, one with Mrs. Ramsay living, the other with Mrs. Ramsay dead. They are united by an interlude called " Time Passes " which covers the whole period of the war ; and each of the three parts is again divided into brief numbered sections. The unity here is of spirit rather than of form. It lies in the texture of thought more than in its arrangement. The two main parts are fitted like two mirrors, the second reflecting the first, fastened together by the hinge of passing time.

But the unity is there. As Mrs. Woolf continues to write, it grows more and more noticeable, affecting quite superficial things such as the recurrence of characters, or far profounder things, intellectual conclusions, preferences, memories. Clarissa and Richard

Dalloway appeared in *The Voyage Out*. There they were younger. Helen Ambrose criticised Clarissa as a thimble-pated chatterer, quite nice, and with moments of heroism, as when, even in a storm, she objected to an untidy bedroom, but tiresome with her " chitter-chatter-chitter-chatter—fish and the Greek alphabet—never listened to a word anyone said—chock-full of idiotic theories about the way to bring up children." Richard was pompous and sentimental, and kissed Rachel after the storm. There are funny discrepancies between the two pictures : in the first, Clarissa is a peer's daughter, fond of music, plays the piano—or so one imagines from her performance of " Tristan " in the cabin, even though she played, with her ringed fingers, only upon the page. In *Mrs. Dalloway* she is, of course, older, more sensible ; her father had been no peer, but a careless, rather unsatisfactory person, Justin Parry, with a country house called Bourton. She cannot play the piano. Her address is not Mayfair but Westminster. Otherwise, she is the same person. To her party come old Mrs. Hilbery, out of *Night and Day* ; Mrs. Durrant and Clarissa from *Jacob's Room* ; Moll Pratt, the flower-woman, has appeared already in *Jacob's Room*. The Parrys appear scattered throughout the novels—Mrs. Raymond Parry in *The Voyage Out*, Mr. Lionel Parry in *Jacob's Room*. Sally Seton becomes Lady Rosseter in *Mrs. Dalloway* ; Miss Rosseter appears in *Jacob's Room*. In *The Voyage Out*, Terence Hewet's aunt writes a Life of Father Damien in English verse ; in *Jacob's Room* an old American lady called Mrs. Duggan performs the same exercise of piety. The Ramsays reflect many characteristics of Helen and Ridley Ambrose. Even in *Orlando* and *A Room of One's Own* the same Nick Greene appears. It is on the whole a rather comfortable habit, making readers feel as though they met old friends among a crowd of strangers.

But the unity is far more profound than anything that can be obtained by a trick of reference. It is metaphysical. The unity which bound Clarissa to Septimus Warren Smith, making her feel that in some way his death was her death, his disgrace her disgrace, his escape a gift to her, is a philosophic unity. She stood by the window when the party was in full swing. " She pulled the blind now. The clock began striking. The young man had killed himself ; but she did not pity him ; with the clock striking the hour, one, two, three, she did not pity him ; with all this going on. There ! the old lady had put out her light ! The whole house was dark now with this going on, she repeated, and the words came to her, ' Fear no more the heat of the sun.' She must go back to them. But what an extraordinary night ! She felt somehow very like him—the young man who had killed himself. She felt glad that he had done it ; thrown it away while they went on living. The clock was striking. The leaden circles dissolved in the air. She must go back. She must assemble. She must find Sally and Peter. And she came in from the little room."

It is a metaphysical unity, the unity which the old scholastic philosophers saw binding creature to creature

and all created things to God. It is also a psychological unity, such as the most modern Viennese
psychologists see binding infancy to age, and making the
whole individual human life a " Recherche du temps
perdu." *To the Lighthouse* opens with little James
Ramsay snubbed and disappointed by his father's
uncompromising insistence upon the truth. He wants
to go to the lighthouse. His father says it will rain.
Charles Tansley backs Mr. Ramsay. Mrs. Ramsay,
endeavouring to protect her son against disappointment
and against truth—as fiercely at war for the moment
with ruthless truth-telling as Ibsen in *The Wild Duck*—
is defeated by the assertive dominance of the men.
Mr. Ramsay snubs her, and at the same time demands
her sympathy. He may pursue truth, but he is, after
all, only a partially successful philosopher with a large
family. " Little James then, as he stood stiff between
her knees, felt her rise in a rosy-flowered fruit tree laid
with leaves and dancing boughs into which the beak of
brass, the arid scimitar of his father, the egotistical man,
plunged and smote, demanding sympathy." Ten
years later, actually sailing, on his way out to the lighthouse with his father, James sits and dreams of a
garden, where flowers grew, and trees, and people
spoke in ordinary voices ; but " something, he remembered, stayed and darkened over him ; would
not move ; something flourished up in the air, something arid and sharp descended even there, like a blade,
a scimitar, smiting through the leaves and flowers,
even of that happy world and making them shrivel
and fall. ' It will rain,' he remembered his father

saying. ' You won't be able to go to the Lighthouse.' "
The old antagonism holds, attracting and repelling.
Youth and childhood and age are bound together. It
is all in accordance with the most up-to-date Freudian
theories.

But unity dwells not only in the history which goes
to make up a single individual. It binds person to
person. Little James Ramsay felt his mother to be
a rosy-flowering fruit tree ; and she herself, gathering
herself together after the effort of coping with her
husband's gloom, " seemed to fold herself together,
one petal closed on another, and the whole fabric fell
in exhaustion upon itself." The symbol which rises in
her son's mind is the same as that which she herself felt.

One reflection after another from the first part of
the novel falls upon the second. Cam Ramsay, the
child, calmed by her mother, when frightened of the
boar's skull, is told that, wrapped in the green shawl,
it looks lovely ; the fairies would love it ; it is like a
bird's nest ; it is like a beautiful mountain, with
valleys and flowers, and bells ringing and birds singing,
and little goats and antelopes. So, right at the end of
the book, on her way to the lighthouse with James and
Ramsay, she falls half asleep and sees the paths and
terraces of the island fading and disappearing. " It
was a hanging garden ; it was a valley, full of birds
and flowers and antelopes "—her mother's reassuring
words.

So, in the first part of the book, Lily Briscoe, painting
her picture of the house in sunlight, used the figure of
Mrs. Ramsay, seated in the window reading to James,

for the shadow she wanted, the triangle of darkness, to balance her composition.

And at the end, trying after ten years to finish the picture, missing Mrs. Ramsay, grieving for Mrs. Ramsay, she looks up and sees Mrs. Ramsay there. The shadow completes the picture. The void is filled. " Mrs. Ramsay—it was part of her perfect goodness to Lily—sat there quite simply, in the chair, flicked her needles to and fro, knitted her reddish-brown stocking, cast her shadow on the step. There she sat." Then " . . . she looked at the steps ; they were empty ; she looked at her canvas ; it was blurred. With a sudden intensity, as if she saw it clear for a second, she drew a line there, in the centre. It was done ; it was finished. Yes, she thought, laying down her brush in extreme fatigue, I have had my vision." But the effect of unity is also partially obtained through the extreme subtlety of Mrs. Woolf's references. It is not merely in arrangement that *Mrs. Dalloway* is built upon the sound of clocks striking and bells ringing. Whenever moments of importance happen in that novel, a bell seems to toll, a clock to strike. There is this about sounds—one cancels out another. The sound of a large bell drowns the sound of a smaller one. So in *Mrs. Dalloway* one incident shuts out another. But light reveals. Mrs. Ramsay is built of light. She herself sees that. " And pausing there, she looked out to meet that stroke of the Lighthouse, the long steady stroke, the last of the three which was her stroke, for watching them in this mood always at this hour, one could not help attaching oneself to one thing especially of the things one saw ; and this thing, the long steady stroke, was her stroke." So in *To the Lighthouse* Mrs. Ramsay, alive or dead gathers and concentrates all thought, all feeling, all action into herself. Her light reveals them. The long steady stroke which is her stroke illumines the island. She *is* the lighthouse, in some subtle way. The action, which in the first half of the book passes through her, is, in the second part, illuminated by her.

But Mrs. Woolf does not achieve her effects only through unity. She can get them from contrast. She can put two and two side by side, and show, with irony and vigour, that they make five—or seventeen, for that matter. There is Peter Walsh in *Mrs. Dalloway* leaving Regent's Park, thinking about Clarissa, thinking that women " don't know what passion is. They don't know the meaning of it to men." And at once, as he crosses the road, a sound interrupts him. It is the old woman singing by Regent's Park Tube Station, singing of love—love which has lasted a million years, " love which prevails, and millions of years ago, her lover who had been dead these centuries, had walked, she crooned, with her in May ; but in the course of ages, long as summer days, and flaming, she remembered, with nothing but red asters, he had gone ; death's enormous sickle had swept those tremendous hills, and when at last she laid her hoary and immensely aged head on the earth, now become a cinder of ice, she implored the gods to lay by her side a bunch of purple heather, there on her high burial place which the last rays of the sun caressed ; for then the pageant of the universe would be over."

The ancient song, Mrs. Woolf declares, bubbled up like a spring, streaming down the pavement all along Marylebone Road. With tenderness and pity and admiration, she transforms the battered, rusty old woman into a thing of beauty, an eternal spring of love and pride and endurance. " Women have no passion," Peter Walsh had thought. Oh, haven't they ? Mrs. Woolf responds. She shows us the old woman. She shows us Rezia Warren Smith. She answers and rebukes Peter Walsh almost before he has time to step into a taxi. Thus, too, does she oppose, in *Jacob's Room,* the sleep of Clara to the wakefulness of Florinda ; in *Mrs. Dalloway,* the order of Clarissa's house to the disorder of Septimus' brain.

Her characters play now a double purpose. They are themselves and they are symbols. They are part of the visible universe and they are its interpretation. Her metaphors have grown more fluid, and they have overflowed into the action of the novel. The motion of time, light, change, the passage of wind through a house, have all assumed a spiritual quality. The section of *To the Lighthouse* called " Time Passes," though ostensibly an account of the Ramsays' empty house on the island, has become a chronicle of human loss, passion, growth and decay.

There is no climax to the books. Even *Mrs. Dalloway* ends before Peter really meets Clarissa at the party. Though in *To the Lighthouse* Mrs. Ramsay at last praises James and Lily finishes her picture,

these are small matters compared to the reconcilia-
tions, weddings, murders and repentances thought
necessary to round off traditional novels. The evasion
worries some readers, as though it were a deliberate
perversity. Deliberate it is certainly ; but there is
more in it than the perverse withdrawal from the
commonplace of a writer seeking peculiarity. Mrs.
Woolf, one feels, is trying to get at a spiritual truth,
and it may be that her own discoveries here have lacked
climax. She may have been drawing from her own
experience when she writes of Lily Briscoe, standing
before her canvas, trying to paint the house after
Mrs. Ramsay's death. " What is the meaning of life ?
That was all—a simple question ; one that tended to
close in on one with years. The great revelation had
never come. The great revelation perhaps never did
come. Instead there were little daily miracles, illu-
minations, matches struck unexpectedly in the dark ;
here was one. This, that, and the other ; herself and
Charles Tansley and the breaking wave ; Mrs. Ramsay
bringing them together ; Mrs. Ramsay saying ' Life
stands still here ' ; Mrs. Ramsay making of the
moment something permanent (as in another sphere
Lily herself tried to make of the moment something
permanent)—this was of the nature of a revelation.
In the midst of chaos there was shape ; this eternal
passing and flowing (she looked at the clouds going
and the leaves shaking) was struck into stability. Life
stands still here, Mrs. Ramsay said. ' Mrs. Ramsay !
Mrs. Ramsay ! ' she repeated. She owed this revelation to her."

The great revelation never comes ; but at any moment the flowing current of life may be struck into permanence if only we see the pattern. " It seemed now as if, touched by human penitence and all its toil, divine goodness had parted the curtain and displayed behind it, single, distinct, the hare erect ; the wave falling ; the boat rocking, which, did we deserve them, should be ours always. But, alas, divine goodness, twitching the cord, draws the curtain ; it does not please him ; he covers his treasures in a drench of hail, and so breaks them, so confuses them that it seems impossible that their calm should ever return or that we should ever compose from their fragments a perfect whole or read in the littered pieces the clear words of truth. For our penitence deserves a glimpse only ; our toil respite only." The glimpses come ; Rachel Vinrace, before her tea-party, saw that " one reached at last this calm, this quiet, this certainty, and it was this process that people called living." Katharine Hilbery looked at Mary Datchet in the twilight and knew at last from the tone of her voice and the little forward shake of her head, " That's how it feels then ; that's how it feels to be in love." Mrs. Dalloway, in the midst of her party, repeated, " Fear no more the heat of the sun." Lily Briscoe saw her picture whole and clear.

These are the moments of revelation which compensate for the chaos, the discomfort, the toil of living. The crown of life is neither happiness nor annihilation : it is understanding. The artist's intuitive vision ; the thinker's slow, laborious approach to truth, climbing through the alphabet of A, B, C, D, up to R, on the long way to Z ; the knowledge that comes to the raw girl, to the unawakened woman—this is life ; this is love. These are the moments in which all the disorder of life assumes a pattern ; we see ; we understand ; and immediately the intolerable burden becomes tolerable ; we stand for a moment on the slopes of that great mountain from the summit of which we can see truth, and thus " enjoy the greatest felicity of which we are capable."

To think this, to believe this, is to rule out of the novel-form the conventionally accepted " happy ending." For marriage, once the postage-stamp fixed on any heroine of fiction to insure her immediate transport to felicity, does not necessarily secure that perception ; sexual satisfaction does not secure it ; the gratification of ambition does not secure it ; Arnold Bennett's dream of a first-class hotel at Brighton does not secure it ; nor the political plumbing of H. G. Wells, with international bath-taps polished, hot and cold water laid on, the Universe Limited scrubbed and disinfected to its last bolt and turncock. The only expedient that will secure it is a certain development and discipline of character. And this, perhaps, is why Mrs. Woolf holds that in novel-writing, character-creation is the all-important quality.

What, then, are they about, these two novels ? What is the subject enclosed in their complex and highly individual forms ? They are about two women, Clarissa Dalloway and Mrs. Ramsay. In both novels there is very little " story," and even very little incident.

Mrs. Dalloway, wife of a Member of Parliament, is about to give a large political reception. While she is preparing for it, Peter Walsh, who had once wanted her to marry him, returns after five years in India and calls upon her. She has an odd little scene with her daughter, who is under the influence of an embittered, frustrated, possessively adoring governess. A shell-shocked neurasthenic, Septimus Warren Smith, married to an Italian wife, is seen in Regent's Park by Peter Walsh, and later, in the evening, when a famous nerve specialist comes to Mrs. Dalloway's party, it is he who has hounded Smith to suicide by his clumsy professional self-assurance. Mrs. Dalloway, the serene, the elegant, the fortunate, feels a moment's sense of intuitive unity and sympathy with the young man who killed himself, then returns to face her party, her exquisite artificial life, and Peter Walsh, whose more natural and adventurous love she still rejects.

To the Lighthouse concerns a house-party on an island off the Hebrides. Here the Ramsays, who are poor but hospitable, invite a number of oddly diverse people to share their summer holidays. When the story opens Mr. Ramsay and his student, Charles Tansley, prophesy that it will be wet next day, so they will not be able to go to the lighthouse—a prophecy deeply resented by the youngest Ramsay child, James. The evening continues ; two of the guests are late for dinner, having become engaged ; the dinner is turned into a little festival of triumph because a dish of *bœuf en daube* turns out a success ; Lily Briscoe the artist leaves her picture of the house unfinished ; they all go to bed. Time passes. Mrs. Ramsay and her eldest daughter die ; a boy is killed in the war. Years later the house-party reassembles. Mr. Ramsay takes James and Cam to the lighthouse—though now they do not wish to go, and Lily Briscoe finishes her picture.

That is all.

Yet the novels contain as much of character-drawing, of moment-creating, of tension and of revelation, as any written in their time. Particularly do they contain two notable portraits of two contrasted women.

Mrs. Dalloway is a complete portrait of the leisured lady. Mrs. Woolf sees the full beauty of that life. Clarissa's education has lain in the refinement of her sensibilities. She is a lady ; she is a hostess ; she is mistress of exquisitely ordered faculties. Her house is her work of art ; it is also her place of discipline. She goes out to buy flowers for her party ; she returns and the maid opens the door for her. " The hall of the house was cool as a vault. Mrs. Dalloway raised her hand to her eyes, and, as the maid shut the door to, and she heard the swish of Lucy's skirts, she felt like a nun who has left the world and feels fold round her the familiar veils and the response to old devotions. The cook whistled in the kitchen. She heard the click of the typewriter. It was her life, and bending her head over the hall table, she bowed beneath the influence, felt blessed and purified, saying to herself, as she took the pad with the telephone message on it, how moments like this are buds on the tree of life,

flowers of darkness they are, she thought (as if some
lovely rose had blossomed for her eyes only) ; not for
a moment did she believe in God ; but all the more,
she thought, taking up the pad, must one repay in daily
life to servants, yes, to dogs and canaries, above all to
Richard her husband, who was the foundation of it.
Of the gay sounds, of the green lights, of the cook even
whistling—for Mrs. Walker was Irish and whistled all
day long—one must pay back from this secret deposit
of exquisite moments, she thought, lifting the pad,
while Lucy stood by her, trying to explain how. . . ."

There she is, with her taste, her fastidiousness, her
courtesies, her snobbery, her desire to be liked, her
parties, her triviality, her humility, her elegance, her
dependence upon her husband. She is growing
older ; life is receding from her. " There was an
emptiness about the heart of life ; an attic room.
Women must put off their rich apparel. At mid-day
they must disrobe. . . . The sheets were clean, tight
stretched in a broad white band from side to side.
Narrower and narrower would her bed be." Her
occupation has been with personal relationships, with
making people like her, arranging flowers and receptions, organising her parties and her house.

Then, as though to show that, lovely and dignified
though Clarissa's life may be, it is imperfect, Mrs. Woolf
makes the man who used to love her, Peter Walsh,
return on the very morning of the party. Peter had
wanted to marry Clarissa, and instead she had chosen
Richard Dalloway, the Conservative Member of
Parliament, chosen to stand at the head of great stair-

cases for receptions, to entertain Prime Ministers, chosen, so Peter thinks, to waste her intelligence, her charm, her beauty. As he runs upstairs and finds her, after five years, in her drawing-room with the inlaid table, the silver, the dolphin, the candlesticks, and all the elaborate equipment of a fashionable hostess, he thinks, " And this has been going on all the time ; week after week ; Clarissa's life ; while I—he thought ; and at once everything seemed to radiate from him ; journeys ; rides ; quarrels ; adventures ; bridge parties ; love affairs ; work ; work ; work ! " He detested the smugness of Clarissa's life, all its proprieties and possessions, and it seems as though Mrs. Woolf had used Peter, with his prejudices and personal motives of chagrin and desire, to say something that is true, to set against the lovely composed picture of Clarissa another standard of values, another way of life. For though Mrs. Woolf can appreciate and even admire the lady of fashion, she knows, she has hinted in *Night and Day*, she makes clear in *A Room of One's Own*, that that way of life means death to the artist, death to reality, death to the full development of intellectual power.

The portrait of Mrs. Ramsay is untouched by such criticism. Mrs. Ramsay has her faults ; she is imperious, quick, impulsive, never has time to carry her desires through into action ; her plans for the mitigation of the human lot remain in her mind, abortive ; she contradicts herself ; she is illogical ; she says " Yea " to life recognising its horror. She " felt this thing that she called life terrible, hostile, and quick to pounce on you if you gave it a chance. There were the eternal problems ; suffering, death, the poor. There was always a woman dying of cancer even here. And yet she had said to all these children, you shall go through with it. To eight people she had said relentlessly that (and the bill for the greenhouse would be fifty pounds) . . . and there she was, she reflected, feeling life rather sinister, making Minta marry Paul Rayley ; because whatever she might feel about her own transaction, and she had had experiences which need not happen to everyone (she did not name them to herself) ; she was driven on, too quickly she knew, almost as if it were an escape for her too, to say that people must marry ; people must have children." But she accepts life ; she accepts the multitudinous claims made upon her by people, by her family and her visitors and the young men gathered about her husband. They overburden her with their demands for sympathy and attention and understanding. One feels that it is the pressure of their demands which shortens her life. Yet it is always towards humanity that she turns. She picks up her basket and goes out, to visit somebody who is ill, to speak to the cook, to do some practical and immediate thing. " And this, like all instincts, was a little distressing to people who did not share it. Her going was a reproach to them, gave a different twist to the world." She had given herself, it seemed, entirely to the world of human beings. Her beauty, so carelessly attired, her nobility, her imperiousness, were perpetually at the service of the community around her. Yet she guarded something secret, a strength, a reticence, which lent dignity to her smallest action, and those whom she served— Lily Briscoe, her children, Charles Tansley—were a little in awe of her. She is, one feels, of all the characters created by Mrs. Woolf, the one most loved by her creator.

Both these women, Mrs. Dalloway and Mrs. Ramsay, the one concerned with elegance, the other concerned with humanity, are shown in relationship to death as well as to life. The theme of *Mrs. Dalloway*, the theme of *To the Lighthouse*, are much the same as the theme of *The Voyage Out* and *Jacob's Room*. What is life ? What is the permanent, tangible thing left over when the flow and surge of time has stilled ?

To reveal this more clearly Mrs. Woolf has shown us Clarissa Dalloway after a severe illness, her hold on life already a little loosened. Sometimes already Clarissa feels hardly real, transparent, almost a ghost, so that she has to look hard at her husband reading his newspaper in order to keep securely attached to life. She is already facing death ; narrower and narrower will her bed be made. She asks herself, " Walking towards Bond Street, did it matter that she must inevitably cease completely ; all this must go on without her ; did she resent it ; or did it not become consoling to believe that death ended absolutely ? but that somehow in the streets of London, on the ebb and flow of things, here, there she survived, Peter survived, lived in each other, she being part, she was positive, of the trees at home, of the house there, ugly, rambling, all to bits and pieces as it was ; part of people she had never met ; being laid out like a mist between the people she knew best, who lifted her on their branches as she had seen the trees lift the mist, but it spread ever so far, her life, herself." She is already detached from that vehement individualism which makes death such a hideous wrench and up-rooting for the young. " She had the oddest sense of being herself invisible, unseen, unknown, there being no more marrying, no more having children now, but only this astonishing and rather solemn progress with the rest of them, up Bond Street. . . . She had a perpetual sense, as she watched the taxi cabs, of being out, out, far out to sea and alone ; she always had the feeling that it was very, very dangerous to live even one day." Already she is, she feels, half out of life, half out of herself : the process of changing from life to death, from death to immortality, which is identifi-cation with life again, has already begun. When alive, she is enclosed in herself, in Clarissa Dalloway ; dead, she will be in the trees and the house and the people, like Wordsworth's Lucy, like Seabrook Flanders, rolled round with rocks and stones and trees.

The theme of *To the Lighthouse* is similar, but Mrs. Woolf has gone one step further. In *Mrs. Dalloway* we are shown Clarissa alive, thinking of death ; in *To the Lighthouse* we are shown Mrs. Ramsay dead, living on through her influence over Cam and James and Mr. Ramsay and Lily Briscoe, absorbed into their life as Clarissa had thought that she would be absorbed. I shall be like a mist upheld by the branches of trees, thought Clarissa. *To the Lighthouse* shows us Mrs. Ramsay upborne on the thoughts of her friends. She asserts herself upon them even after Lily thinks she has gone for ever. " ' Oh, the dead ! ' she murmured ; one pitied them, one brushed them aside, one had even a little contempt for them. They are at our mercy. . . . For a moment Lily, standing there, with the sun hot on her back, triumphed over Mrs. Ramsay."

The moment of her triumph is followed by loss. Lily stands on the lawn before her unfinished picture, unable to find comfort anywhere, even in painting, because of the empty place on the steps where Mrs. Ramsay once sat. Silently, she summons her, believing somehow that if she asserts her will, if she joins with old Mr. Carmichael who sits silent there on the lawn, and calls Mrs. Ramsay back, she will return and fill the space, revive the beauty. She calls ; her memories stream in upon her ; she watches the sailing-boat carrying Mr. Ramsay and Cam and James out to the lighthouse ; she remembers a thousand things : Mrs. Ramsay vexed because some one was late, or a teapot chipped ; her preoccupation with human beings ; her relationship with her husband ; and suddenly, even as she longs and remembers, Mrs. Ramsay returns. Her presence takes its place in the window, completes the design ; the ephemeral is stabilised ; the transient becomes permanent ; the picture is finished. Yes, says Lily, I have had my vision. That is the end.

Thus *To the Lighthouse* is a ghost story. Its characters move in a radiant, half-transparent atmosphere, as though already suffused into the spiritual world. The action takes place out at sea, on an island ; because it is there, away from the land, on a ship, out at sea, on an island, that Mrs. Woolf sees humanity with detachment. From that vantage point she can look back on life, look back on death, and write her parable. Its quality is poetic ; its form and sub-stance are perfectly fused, incandescent, disciplined into unity. It is a parable of life, of art, of experience ; it is a parable of immortality. It is one of the most beautiful novels written in the English language.

VIII
TWO IN A TAXI

THE significance of *To the Lighthouse* was tragic. Its analysis was luminous and profound, its mood poetic, its preoccupations spiritual. It concerned life and death and human character. Those who read and admired it awaited eagerly its successor, expecting another Clarissa Dalloway, another Mrs. Ramsay. They got, in 1928, *Orlando : a Biography* ; in 1929, *A Room of One's Own.*

Both books were disconcerting. Neither was of the kind that Mrs. Woolf had been expected to write. The first was a brilliant, high-spirited, erudite fantasia on an odd historical theme ; the second an essay on the position of women. But the form and the subjects of the books caused more surprise than they really justified. They concerned matters which had always interested Mrs. Woolf, and revealed an attitude which she had already shown in her former writings. Literature, time and sex were not newly acquired interests, and both her new books were concerned with these.

Different as they are in form, the two books are complementary. *Orlando* dramatises the theories stated more plainly in the essay. The essay makes clear the meaning of the allegory. That is why it seems expedient to examine the two together.

Orlando is a fantasy. It is prefaced by a dedication and a gently ridiculous introduction, satirising the

L

solemn preludes to similar, more serious works, thanking a long list of helpers whose identity reveals to some extent Mrs. Woolf's literary ancestry and associates : Defoe, Sir Thomas Browne, Sterne, Sir Walter Scott, Lord Macaulay, Emily Brontë, De Quincey, Walter Pater, Madame Lopokova, Roger Fry, Julian Bell, Janet Case, Adrian Stephen, Francis Birrell, G. H. Rylands, Harold Nicholson, Madame Jacques Raverat, and numbers more—" but the list threatens to grow too long and is already far too distinguished."

That Mrs. Woolf should write a fantasy was not at all surprising. She had already, in *A Society*, shown how well she could design a light-hearted squib. In *To the Lighthouse* she had enjoyed Mrs. Ramsay's gift of extravagant speech. Mrs. Ramsay cried that she would not keep dinner waiting for the Queen of England, " not for the Empress of Mexico." It was, after all, only going one step further to make Orlando actually late for dinner with a queen. Mrs. Woolf had in *A Society* described the girl Rose going aboard one of His Majesty's ships disguised as an Ethiopian prince ; it was only going one step further to make the woman Orlando actually to have been British Ambassador at Constantinople. She had, in all her books, played with the notion of time and its importance. In *Mrs. Dalloway* the whole significance of fifty years had been gathered into twenty-four hours ; it was only going one step further, in *Orlando*, to spread the experience of some forty years out over three centuries.

The story itself opens with a picture of Orlando, as a young gallant of the Elizabethan age, practising swordsmanship in the attic rooms of a great country house. He is a handsome, clever, sullen, solitary boy, given to meditation and the writing of poetry, loving the country and the great park lands enclosing his father's handsome house. He wanders off to a hill under an oak tree, from which can be seen " nineteen English counties . . . and on clear days thirty or perhaps forty, if the weather was very fine." The Queen arrives ; Orlando is late to serve her ; but handsome ; and is received into her favour, which he too soon loses by letting himself be seen in the act of kissing a lady-in-waiting ; he retires, but reappears at the court of King James ; falls in love there ; is cheated by a Russian princess, again retires, takes to the writing of poetry, entertains a guest from Fleet Street called Nick Greene, finds himself, as reward, held up to mockery (it being now, somehow or other, the late seventeenth century, and the Grub Street school in process of formation) ; sets himself to the furnishing of his house, is pursued by an amorous Archduchess, and takes honourable flight, as Ambassador Extraordinary, to Constantinople.

There, after a brief period of brilliant distinction, culminating in abundant honours and a dukedom, he falls asleep, and on awakening, stands upright in complete nakedness, a woman. As a woman, she flies to the gipsies, finds that her perverse artistic and intellectual awareness builds a barrier between her and quite simple people, returns to England during the eighteenth century, to wander again through her great house, to rediscover the Archduchess as an Archduke, and to entertain Mr. Pope and Mr. Swift and Mr. Addison, and to wander untrammelled about London, until the nineteenth century begins.

And with the nineteenth century, London changes, England changes, Orlando changes. As the ivy clings more abundantly to her house, she yearns for a husband on whom to lean. At the right moment, in circumstances appropriately romantic, she encounters a gentleman called Marmaduke Bonthrop Shelmerdine, Esquire, who spends his time in riding great horses or sailing round Cape Horn (singularly like the dreamlover of Katharine Hilbery). She loves him, marries him, bids him farewell on his adventures, completes her poem *The Oak Tree*, carries it off to London, where she is patronised by Nick Greene, now become Sir Nicholas and enormously respectable ; she studies Victorian literature ; she bears a son and heir ; and later—it being now October 1928 (the month in which Mrs. Woolf herself was reading papers on " Women and Fiction " at Newnham and Girton)—she goes to Marshall & Snelgrove's to buy linen sheets for the great double-bed. There she encounters the Russian Princess, now grown old, fat, and the mistress of a Grand Duke. She drives herself home in her car, rejoicing in her fame, for *The Oak Tree* has won a prize, in her sons, her house, in the grounds through which, on arriving home, she wanders ; but her joy is incomplete, for her husband is sailing round Cape Horn. Night descends. She remembers her past ;

her fleeting glimpse of Shakespeare, and the visit of the Queen.

But with the roar of the wind and the return of the present, comes an aeroplane ; and as from it Shelmerdine, now grown a fine sea-captain, hale, fresh-coloured, and alert, leapt to the ground, there sprang up over his head a single wild bird.

" ' It is the goose ! ' Orlando cried. ' The wild goose. . . .'

" And the twelfth stroke of midnight sounded ; the twelfth stroke of midnight, Thursday, the eleventh of October, nineteen hundred and twenty-eight."

Such a story is notably full of extravagances. It deals with a poet who grew only forty years older in over three hundred years, who changed sex half-way through life, who did a preposterous number of things and knew an impossible number of people. What was still more odd, the book being dedicated to a living poet, V. Sackville West, was called " A Biography," and the first edition was illustrated by photographs of its heroine and portraits of her ancestors. Identification was obvious and deliberate. Any reader who felt curious could turn to *Who's Who* and the current press and learn there that the Honourable Victoria Sackville West was a daughter of Lord Sackville, that she had been brought up at Knole, one of the most famous of great English country houses, that she had married the Honourable Harold Nicholson, once a member of the British diplomatic service, himself also a writer and critic ; that she had two sons ; had travelled in the East, and had won the Hawthornden

Prize with her poem " The Land," so shamelessly quoted as " The Oak Tree " in *Orlando*. In short, *Orlando* was not merely called a biography. It was one. But it was a composite biography. It concerned not only V. Sackville West, the twentieth-century poet, but her ancestors. And this was not through any casual and humorous whim of Mrs. Woolf's. The choice arose from the first stage of that argument on literature, time and sex which runs through the two books, *Orlando* and *A Room of One's Own*, and which can be traced, in scattered fragments, throughout Mrs. Woolf's other novels and critical work.

Literature, Mrs. Woolf had said in *Mr. Bennett and Mrs. Brown* and *The Common Reader*, and was to repeat in *A Room of One's Own*, is a composite production. The individual artist does not stand alone. He draws life from his forerunners, as his successors will draw life from him. " Without those forerunners," she says in *A Room of One's Own*, " Jane Austen and the Brontës and George Eliot could no more have written than Shakespeare could have written without Marlowe, or Marlowe without Chaucer, or Chaucer without those forgotten poets who paved the ways and tamed the natural savagery of the tongue. For masterpieces are not single and solitary births ; they are the outcome of many years of thinking in common."

Believing that, confirming her belief by a wide knowledge of the history of literature, there was nothing perverse nor extravagant in her design to write a composite biography of a poet. There was a poem, " The Land," grave, classical, assured, owing much to Virgil, something to the Elizabethans, something to Thompson, a trifle, perhaps, to Wordsworth. There was a poet, Victoria Sackville West, whose debt to her ancestors was written across her handsome, proud, intelligent features, which reproduced so strikingly the features of men and women in the portraits hung in the great galleries of Knole. It was from them that she had inherited a taste for solitary contemplation, independence, intelligence and the self-confidence necessary for an artist to complete his work. When one thought of a poet, who was a person, one had to think also of all the various ancestors who had contributed to his heredity. Regarded from one aspect, *Orlando* is a dramatised history of literary fashion.

It opens in the Elizabethan age—an opening most natural for Mrs. Woolf, who had fallen in love with that period, and who so obviously enjoyed writing about it. When she resumed the argument in *A Room of One's Own*, it was with Shakespeare's imaginary sister that her survey of women's contribution to literature began. But really, so far as Orlando was concerned, it was an arbitrary choice. Had Mrs. Woolf been concerned purely with academic values, she should have traced the literary ancestry of " The Land " back to Virgil's exile. But she decided to deal with the poet rather than the poem, with a picture seen at Knole, and with the Elizabethan age. So she shows how Orlando wrote enormous tragedies in which Vice, Crime, Misery and other abstract personalities abounded ; kings and queens ruled impossible territories, horrid plots confounded and noble sentiments suffused them. All was grandiloquent, immense and luscious. Mrs. Woolf adapts her story to her subject. The Queen is as spectacular and grotesque a figure as one might wish ; her rages are royal, her favours overwhelming. The extravagance of the period is matched by the extravagance of Mrs. Woolf's hyperbole : " The age was the Elizabethan ; the morals were not ours ; nor their poets ; nor their climate ; nor their vegetables even. Everything was different. . . . The brilliant amorous day was divided as sheerly from the night as land from water. Sunsets were redder and more intense ; dawns were whiter and more auroral. Of our crepuscular half-lights and lingering twilights they knew nothing."

But from the profusion of that abundant epoch, Orlando passed on to the late seventeenth and eighteenth centuries. His exuberance was tamed by the classical severity of the age of reason, just as the precision of form, the eclogue style, the classical tranquillity of " The Land " had come to V. Sackville West from Virgil's Italy, seen through the spy-glass of the age of Pope and Dryden. Then Orlando wrote tragedies called *The Death of Ajax* or *The Birth of Pyramus*. His drawers were stuffed with manuscripts, not one of which " lacked the name of some mythological personage at a crisis in his career."

It was then that he began to write *The Oak Tree, a Poem*. " His floridity was chastened ; his abundance curbed ; the age of prose was congealing those warm fountains." He interrupted his composition to go East, and to change his sex. It was the Lady Orlando, living in the eighteenth century, who resumed it. But she, too, was subject to interruptions. She entertained Swift, Pope and Dryden ; she pursued her studies of life round Leicester Square. And the nineteenth century closed in upon her before the poem was more than well begun. And with the nineteenth century, England changed again ; literature changed.

" Stealthily and imperceptibly, none marking the exact day or hour of the change, the constitution of England was altered and nobody knew it. Everywhere the effects were felt. The hardy country gentleman, who had sat down gladly to a meal of ale and beef in a room designed, perhaps by the brothers Adam, with classic dignity, now felt chilly. Rugs appeared ; beards were grown ; trousers were fastened right under the instep. The chill which he felt in his legs the country gentleman soon transferred to his house ; furniture was muffled ; walls and tables were covered ; nothing was left bare. Then a change of diet became essential. The muffin was invented and the crumpet. Coffee supplanted the after-dinner port, and, as coffee led to a drawing-room in which to drink it, and a drawing-room to glass cases, and glass cases to artificial flowers, and artificial flowers to mantelpieces, and mantelpieces to pianofortes, and pianofortes to drawing-room ballads, and drawing-room ballads (skipping a stage or two) to innumerable little dogs, mats and china ornaments, the home—which had become extremely important—was completely altered. . . . But the change did not stop at outward things. . . . The sexes drew further and further apart. No open conversation was tolerated. . . . The life of the average woman was a succession of childbirths. She married at nineteen and had fifteen or eighteen children by the time she was thirty ; for twins abounded. Thus the British Empire came into existence ; and thus—for there is no stopping damp ; it gets into the inkpot as it gets into the woodwork—sentences swelled, adjectives multiplied, lyrics became epics, and little trifles that had been essays a column long were now encyclopædias in ten or twenty volumes. . . . Giant cauliflowers towered deck above deck. . . . Hens laid incessantly eggs of no special tint. . . . The whole sky itself as it spread wide above the British Isles was nothing but a vast feather-bed ; and the undistinguished fecundity of the garden, the bedroom, and the hen-roost was copied there."

And with the English temperament and constitution, Orlando's style changed absolutely, " began to curve and caracole with the smoothest possible fluency. Her page was written in the neatest sloping Italian hand with the most insipid verse she had ever read in her life :

> " I am myself but a vile link
> Amid life's weary chain,
> But I have spoken hallow'd words,
> Oh, do not say in vain !

> " Will the young maiden, when her tears
> Alone in moonlight shine,
> Tears for the absent and the loved,
> Murmur . . ."

Or again—

> " She was so changed, the soft carnation cloud
> Once mantling o'er her cheek like that which eve
> Hangs o'er the sky, glowing with roseate hue,
> Had faded into paleness, broken by
> Bright burning blushes, torches of the tomb."

It was not until some time, one imagines in the twentieth century, after she had married and Shelmerdine had left her to sail round the Horn, that she took up her pen and wrote what Victoria Sackville West actually did write :

> " And then I came to a field where springing grass
> Was dulled by the hanging cups of fritillaries,
> Sullen and foreign looking, the snaky flower,
> Scarfed in dull purple, like Egyptian girls —"

Even then she had doubts about it. " When she had written " Egyptian girls " the power told her to stop. Grass, the power seemed to say, going back with a ruler such as governesses use to the beginning, is all right ; the hanging cups of fritillaries—admirable ; the snaky flower—a thought strong from a lady's pen, perhaps, but Wordsworth, no doubt, sanctions it ; but—girls ? Are girls necessary ? You have a husband at the Cape you say ? Ah, well, that'll do. And so the spirit passed on."

Orlando escaped. " She had just managed by some dexterous deference to the spirit of the age, by putting on a ring and finding a man on the moor, by loving nature and being no satirist, cynic or psychologist . . . to pass its examination successfully."

Orlando escaped. The time-spirit which bore so hardly upon women poets had not, by the twentieth century, irreparably damaged her. But during her fantastic pilgrimage she had evaded dangers which might well have overwhelmed one less gifted and less privileged. For Mrs. Woolf's contention, dramatised in *Orlando* and further discussed in *A Room of One's Own*, is that since literature is a composite production, the notebooks of one generation providing material for masterpieces in the next, is subject to fashions and influences. Its character changes, in spite of the individuality of the poet's personal vision. Contemporary morals, manners and social institutions affect it.

That appears to be the first stage in the argument. But the second follows. If circumstances and manners can affect literature, so also can economic conditions. In the fantasy, by making Orlando lord of a great estate, and at one time even a duke, Mrs. Woolf enables herself to take wealth and leisure for granted. But it is, I think, a very deliberate choice. For in the essay she shows what happened to writers who had not these privileges. She observed George Eliot and Jane Austen and the Brontës, and saw that they lacked privacy, security and command of their own leisure. With vivid cogency she draws a picture of what might have happened to herself had she possessed no independent income. This imaginary self had, she said, earned her living in a dozen of the harsh and ineffective ways open before 1918 to untrained women. " Cadging odd jobs from newspapers, by reporting a donkey show here or a wedding there ; I had earned a few pounds by addressing envelopes, reading to old ladies, making artificial flowers, teaching the alphabet to small children in a kindergarten. . . . But what still remains with me as a worse infliction . . . was the poison of fear and bitterness which those days bred in me. To begin with, always to be doing work which one did not wish to do, and to do it like a slave, flattering and fawning, not always necessarily perhaps, but it seemed necessary and the stakes were too great to run risks ; and then the thought of that one gift which it was death to hide—a small one but dear to the possessor —perishing and with it my self, my soul—all this became like a rust eating away the bloom of the spring, destroying the tree at its heart." Then came a legacy. " It is remarkable," Mrs. Woolf observes, " what a change of temper a fixed income will bring about. No force in the world can take from me my five hundred pounds. Food, house and clothing are mine for ever. Therefore not merely do effort and labour cease, but also hatred and bitterness. I need not hate any man ; he cannot hurt me. I need not flatter any man ; he has nothing to give me. So imperceptibly I found myself adopting a new attitude towards the other half of the human race. . . . Indeed, my aunt's legacy unveiled the sky to me, and substituted for the large and imposing figure of a gentleman, which Milton recommended for my perpetual adoration, a view of the open sky." Marx himself has hardly put the materialistic interpretation of psychology more clearly.

It is necessary then to have a reasonable income in

order to write fully without fear or favour. But women have, Mrs. Woolf declares, throughout history, remained poor. They have remained ignorant. They have remained in an inferior position. It has been, indeed, to the interests of men to keep them so. Life for both sexes, Mrs. Woolf observes, is a difficult struggle, and only those survive who can preserve their self-confidence. But the surest way to do this is to feel superior when others clearly are inferior. If all men could keep all women in an inferior position, feeling inferior, the thing was done. " Women have served all these centuries as looking-glasses possessing the magic and delicious power of reflecting the figure of man at twice its natural size. Without that power probably the earth would still be swamp and jungle. . . ." The mirrors are especially necessary in less civilised society when violent and heroic action must be taken. " That is why Napoleon and Mussolini both insist so emphatically upon the inferiority of women, for if they were not inferior, they would cease to enlarge." Men have therefore endeavoured to keep their mirrors, and women have submitted, until most of them are incapable of reflecting their world candidly at its proper size. The idea is not new to Mrs. Woolf. In *The Voyage Out* Hewet says to Rachel, " The respect that women, even well-educated, very able women, have for men, . . . never ceases to amaze me. . . . I believe we must have the sort of power over you that we're said to have over horses. They see us three times as big as we are, or they'd never obey us."

The importance of this inequality of position lies in

its effect upon the productive power of women artists. If women were crippled by poverty, by subordination, by lack of means and of leisure, they could not even see the truth. They were isolated from reality, and part of reality, which they alone could see, would remain unrevealed.

But truth is necessary to human development. Cut off from contact with reality, we walk dwarfed and crippled. Whatever other obligation is laid upon us, this is imperative—to discern the truth, to extend our knowledge of reality.

The time has come, Mrs. Woolf at last discovered, when in order to proceed further along the road to truth, we must demand the co-operation of women, and persuade them to make their contribution. But how can this be done ? What is it that women need in order to liberate them from their ancient handicaps, to enable them to reveal whatever they can reveal of truth ? She answered, in her essay, " Five hundred a year and a room of one's own."

She is driven, then, for the first time, to a conclusion which is something new in her work. The consideration of ends is no longer adequate. Always, hitherto, in the recurrent debate between artist and politician, she had been on the side of the artist. She preferred things that were ends in themselves. She " preferred Shakespeare." Now she realises that Shakespeare may have had a sister whose work has been lost to the world because the circumstances which might have made it possible were lacking. She is driven to the politicians' argument, driven to concern herself with the external arrangements of the world—with writing cheques and joining societies, and making protests, and doing all those things which must be done before women can go to college, can achieve adequate education, can enter professions which provide them with a handsome income, can obtain freedom and self-assurance to look at life. *Orlando* and *A Room of One's Own* between them have swung her right round into considerations of economics and social customs, and plans and institutions. It is not without significance, considering her frequent protests against protest, that when Oxford women undergraduates sent out an appeal for funds to found a combined club for themselves, they headed their appeal with the name of Mrs. Woolf's essay.

Does all this mean, then, that the truth which men see is completely different from truth seen by women ? To judge from many modern writers we might indeed think that men and women inhabited different worlds, black and white, sixes and sevens, meaning different things for the two sexes. Does Mrs. Woolf want us to make it possible for women to be artists because sex indeed strikes a dividing line from Heaven down to the roots of the earth, with all men on one side and all women on the other ? " Women's world," " women's interests," " women's tastes," " women's brains," say the contemporary newspapers, magazines, advertisements. Does she share the fashionable belief in complete and unalterable division ?

And here we come to the third part of the argument, and the significance of the central puzzle in *Orlando*,

its most distinctive and original trick of fantasy. In
the middle of the story Orlando changes her sex. The
Elizabethan gallant, the lover of Sasha, the patron of
Nick Greene, the Ambassador to Constantinople, was
a man. But the creature who awoke after the riots in
Constantinople was a woman. Mrs. Woolf is quite clear
about it. Why? What did she mean by it? Why
introduce this curious extravagance into a learned
parable of literary criticism? It is possibly true that
certain quite minor motives helped to direct her
imagination. The Sackville portraits in which one
can trace the features of V. Sackville West are at first
those of men, later of women. Clearly the modern
writer inherited from both the male and female line.
As we all do.

There was another thing. If we trace the course
of literature, the early stream runs almost entirely
through male channels, because, for reasons which
Mrs. Woolf shows in *A Room of One's Own*, it was
uncommonly difficult for women to write plays, to
write poetry, to write, indeed, at all. As a matter of
convenience, as well as a matter of history, it was easier
to show Orlando as a man until at least after Aphra
Behn had written. If he was to be a poet, a man he
must be. But Mrs. Woolf was interested in women.
She believed in the capacities of women. Miss Sackville West was herself a woman. After the return from
Constantinople, then, Orlando should be a woman.
Given this historical argument, the fact of the change,
its method, the pageant of the virtues by which it
was accompanied, all the entertaining and satirical

and delicious decoration by which her fancy surrounded it, were merely devices of that taste for hyperbole which she had shown elsewhere in her novels.

But she also makes Orlando change from man to woman in order to pursue her own particular theory of the sexes.

And here one is handicapped by the confusing effect of social influence upon the English language. We ought, when talking about the difference between men and women, to be allowed to use some such neutral word as " gender " instead of " sex." For " sex " has been associated so closely with the amorous and procreative instinct, that its convenience has been destroyed, and its meaning lent an emotional significance which may be quite alien to our purpose. Especially is this true when dealing with a mind like Mrs. Woolf's, so sensitive to fine distinctions and so precise in its conceptions.

The difference between men and women is so obviously a matter of importance, in literature as well as life, that it is not surprising to find many hundreds of thousands of pages devoted to its discussion. Mrs. Woolf's particular theory, which enabled her to change Orlando from a man to a woman with so remarkably little fuss, is expounded more deliberately in the essay, and especially in a passage where she describes her sensations while watching a man and a girl climb into a taxi and drive off together. " The sight," she says, " was ordinary enough ; what was strange was the rhythmical order with which my imagination had invested it ; and the fact that the ordinary sight of two people getting into a cab had the power to communicate something of their own seeming satisfaction. . . . Perhaps to think, as I had been thinking these two days, of one sex as distinct from the other is an effort. It interferes with the unity of the mind. Now that effort had ceased and that unity had been restored by seeing two people come together and get into a taxicab. . . . The satisfaction it gave me made me also ask whether there are two sexes in the mind corresponding to the two sexes in the body, and whether they also require to be united in order to get complete satisfaction and happiness ? " She goes on to sketch a plan of the soul, presided over by two powers, male and female ; in a man, the male predominates, and in a woman, the female, the normal and healthy state being when the two live in harmony together. " If one is a man, still the woman part of the brain must have effect ; and a woman must also have intercourse with the man in her. Coleridge perhaps meant this when he said that a great mind is androgynous. It is when this fusion takes place that the mind is fully fertilised and uses all its faculties. Perhaps a mind that is purely masculine cannot create, any more than a mind that is purely feminine. It is fatal to be a man or woman pure and simple ; one must be woman-manly or man-womanly."

There is the theory, stated as clearly and unambiguously as she could state it. Having read that, we can return to *Orlando* and find its meaning more obvious. " The difference between the sexes," writes Mrs. Woolf there, " is, happily, one of great profundity.

Clothes are but a symbol of something hid deep beneath. . . . Here again, we come to a dilemma. Different though the sexes are, they intermix. In every human being a vacillation from one sex to the other takes place, and often it is only the clothes that keep the male or female likeness, while underneath the sex is the very opposite of what it is above." With Orlando the confusion arose because sometimes the male and sometimes the female side was uppermost and she (or he) dressed to suit her (or his) mind. But, being a creature of fantasy, growing only thirty years older in three hundred years, she was also able to change her physical anatomy with her clothes, the physical anatomy being, according to Mrs. Woolf, who here differs profoundly from most other modern writers, a matter of small importance.

She does not simplify life by saying that sex is unimportant. She proclaims its importance, but denies the implications usually derived from its significance. " Then consider the effect of sex," she says in *Jacob's Room*, " how between man and woman it hangs wavy, tremulous, so that here's a valley, there's a peak, where in truth, perhaps, all's as flat as my hand." People see the line drawn between men and women, and rule their lives according to the sight. There is indeed, Mrs. Woolf has repeatedly declared, a masculine world and a feminine world. Terence Hewet's criticism of St. John Hirst and his career ; the conspiracy of young women in *A Society* ; the definition of masculine values in *The Mark on the Wall* ; Peter Walsh's comparison of his own activities with Clarissa's ; Mrs. Woolf's own comparison of Jacob's world and Clara Durrant's ; Katharine Hilbery's discovery in Kew Gardens of the joy of Ralph's masculine conversation—all these indications convey to us her impression of the man-dominated and woman-dominated worlds.

But there are two in the taxi. And all through her work Mrs. Woolf has recognised this at least by implication. Katharine and Cassandra in *Night and Day* represented very well, she tells us, " the manly and the womanly sides of the feminine nature." Mrs. Dalloway, the lady of fashion, who has devoted her life almost exclusively to the cultivation of her feminine nature, yet harbours unexpelled the masculine tenant of her mind. Thinking of her own lack of passion and response to the demands of men she remembers that she could not resist sometimes yielding to the charm of " a woman, not a girl, of a woman confessing, as to her they often did, some scrape, some folly. And whether it was pity or their beauty, or that she was older, or some accident—like a faint scent or a violin next door. . . she did undoubtedly then feel what men feel, only for a moment ; but it was enough. . . . But this question of love . . . this falling in love with women. Take Sally Seton ; her relation in the old days with Sally Seton. Had not that, after all, been love ? " The Ramsay girls thought of the Bank of England and the Indian Empire, of ringed fingers and lace, and these old symbols of responsibility and prestige " called out the manliness of their girlish hearts."

Mrs. Woolf, then, makes her own characters manly-womanly and womanly-manly. Her women may not all have been men once, as Orlando was, but they harbour a hidden man within their hearts. Thus, though the sexes differ, they do not estrange. Once inside the taxi of human personality, man and woman can instruct each other. The man within Mrs. Woolf's heart had taught her many things. It was he, presumably, who had enabled her to draw with such assurance her portraits of young men. Jane Austen, like Mrs. Woolf, had lived in a household with young men ; but she preferred to show her male characters almost always in relationship to women. We hardly ever find them talking together, as Terence Hewet and St. John Hirst talk, as William Rodney, Ralph Denham and Henry Otway talk, as the young men talk in *Jacob's Room*. Mrs. Woolf has dared to do this because she has not only observed young men. She has shared something with them. The manliness in her heart proclaims her kinship.

Her immediate statement of the problem presents difficulties. They are, possibly, superficial difficulties arising from our poverty of language and our ignorance of secondary sexual characteristics. When the physical differences of men and women have been discussed and dismissed, she still retains the terms " male " and " female " for psychological attributes. And here an obstacle arises.

For we have to fix the labels after an intellectual process which at its best is guesswork. We cannot recognise infallibly what characteristics beyond those

which are purely physical are " male " and " female."
Custom and prejudice, history and tradition have
designed the fashion plates ; we hardly know yet what
remains beneath them of the human being. When
writers like D. H. Lawrence and Wyndham Lewis talk
about " masculine values " and " a masculine world "
we can guess pretty much what they mean. When
Mrs. Woolf in *The Mark on the Wall* speaks of " the
masculine point of view which governs our lives," she
herself hints at its secret in Whitaker's Table of
Precedency. She draws two recognisable pictures of
a " feminine " novel and a " masculine " novel in
A Room of One's Own. She speaks of the special
creativeness of women. Yet looking round upon the
world of human beings as we know it, we are hard put
to it to say what is the natural shape of men or women,
so old, so all-enveloping are the moulds fitted by
history and custom over their personalities. We do
not know how much of sensitiveness, intuition, pro-
tectiveness, docility and tenderness may not be
naturally " male," how much of curiosity, aggression,
audacity and combativeness may not be " female."
Which part of Orlando was it that made her write
The Oak Tree, cry " Ecstasy " in the park, fall in love
and out again with Sasha in Marshall & Snelgrove's ?
We do not know. We might as well call the con-
flicting strains within the human personality black and
white, negative and positive, as male and female. The
time has not yet come when we can say for certain
which is the man and which the woman, after both
have boarded the taxi of human personality.

But the time has come when we can say something certainly, and Mrs. Woolf has said it. "It is fatal," she declared at the end of *A Room of One's Own*, "for anyone who writes to think of their sex. It is fatal to be a man or woman pure and simple ; one must be woman-manly or man-womanly. Some collaboration has to take place in the mind between the woman and the man before the art of creation can be accomplished. Some marriage of opposites has to be consummated. The whole of the mind must lie wide open if we are to get the sense that the writer is communicating his experience with perfect fulness. There must be freedom and there must be peace. . . . All this pitting of sex against sex, of quality against quality ; all this claiming of superiority and imparting of inferiority, belong to the private school stage of human existence where there are ' sides ' and it is necessary for one side to beat the other side. . . . As people mature they cease to believe in sides."

To the mature human being, then, this matter of maleness and femaleness becomes unimportant. Variety matters ; integrity matters ; understanding matters ; but which shape of body holds which type of mind becomes really very unimportant.

This doctrine of the sexes is not quite peculiar to Mrs. Woolf, though no one, perhaps, has dramatised it so effectively, nor explained it with such confidence. Coleridge believed in the androgynous mind of poets ; William Blake upheld faith in Being which transcended sex. He looked to a future when "sexes shall vanish and cease to be" and regarded a present in which male and female intermingled.

" For Los said :
  ' When the Individual appropriates universality
  He divides into Male and Female, and when the
    Male and Female
  Appropriate Individuality they become an Eternal
    Death.' "

That division means eternal death is implicit in all Mrs. Woolf's writing. It underlies her doctrine of love, which, by creating unity, facilitates understanding. And understanding is life. The complete human being, the artist, is cut off from reality by no accident of sex, and the knowledge of reality is the really important thing. The difficulty of sex-differentiation is overcome by taking as criterion some measure of value greater than the measure of sexual difference. That criterion is the relationship of the individual to reality—a relationship which men and women share alike. By concentrating on intellectual likeness instead of physiological difference, she achieves her knowledge of unity. It is a knowledge achieved by all great mystics and poets. The barriers dividing man from man, man from God, sex from sex, race from race and class from class have become transparent and dissolved in the light of reality. Past and present, time and space, colour and sound, contingent and absolute have flowed together. Light answers shade ; death answers life ; the fears, hatreds and misunderstandings of division disappear.

IX
" THE WAVES "—AND AFTER ?

IN 1931 Mrs. Woolf published two revealingly diverse
pieces of work—her Introduction to *Life as We Have
Known it*, a series of biographical sketches written
by members of the Women's Co-operative Guild, and
her novel *The Waves*. The former marks her furthest
excursion into political writing. It continues the
argument running through *A Society*, *Orlando*, *A
Room of One's Own*, and some of the critical essays,
recognising the part played, even in the artist's life,
by the practical, material conditions of living. The
novel is the most delicate, complex and aesthetically
pure piece of writing that she has yet produced.

It has been conceived, not only in the mood, but
in the manner of poetry. It had been designed, one
feels, as an organic whole. It fulfils the conditions
postulated for poetry in an essay by Professor Alexander, published in November 1931, which seems
very happily to describe this distinction. " In the
poem," he says, " the subject as rendered in words . . .
acquires a life of its own, is a living thing, as it were,
living its own life like an animal or plant, is organic
. . . while prose, for all its constructive unity, is not
self-subsistent but is descriptive of a given subject . . .
It is that the poet places himself within the subject
itself and works from within outwards, while the
prosaist describes relatively, from without. The poet

starts with the subject in its integrity, places the
hearer's mind within it, and his exposition is the un-
folding life of the subject itself." The distinction
does not seem to me to hold good for all prose and
all poetry. I should want to place the *Æneid* and
Paradise Lost on the side of Professor Alexander's
prose and *The Waves* on the side of his poetry. But
he does say something important. His definition
does, I think, explain how, fundamentally, *The Waves*
differs from the traditional English novel.

Its theme is similar to that of *The Voyage Out*,
Jacob's Room, and *To the Lighthouse*. It concerns
the preparation of the individual for life and death
and the effect of death upon survivors. Its external
action is slight ; its " story " tenuous and its " plot "
almost non-existent. Six children, Bernard, Neville,
Louis, Susan, Jinny and Rhoda, are brought together
to share governesses in a country house by the sea.
They already display, in the first episode of their
childhood, the fates which, being ingrained in their
own personalities, are to pursue them through their
lives. Bernard already is sociable, malleable, sympathises with and comforts Susan—who loves him, but
whom he never specially loves—he already makes
phrases, lives in the hour, enters the joys and griefs of
others, and hardly knows, among so varied and shifting
a cloud of sensations, which is himself. Neville is
already precise, fastidious, finding in the distinctions
of his grammar-lesson the introduction to an ordered
universe. Louis is already struggling against his
sense of inferiority, because his father, a banker in

Brisbane, failed, because he has an Australian accent, because he does not feel himself to be quite a gentleman. Susan is passionate, possessive, loving and hating ; Jinny already dances, febrile and mischievous, and kisses Louis under the trees ; Rhoda, shy, withdrawn, cannot do her lessons, and dreams apart, rocking flower-petal boats in a basin.

The six grow up. The three boys go to school together and acquire there a gorgeous, unconscious, Olympian friend called Percival. The girls go to school together and acquire nothing but a sense of soap, pine, and superimposed order. They pass on, Neville and Bernard to Cambridge, Louis to an office ; Jinny and Rhoda to the life of a debutante, Susan back to her father's country vicarage. There is a party in a London restaurant where they all meet to say goodbye to Percival, who is going to India, to do great things there, they all feel, for he is a natural leader. He loves Susan ; Neville and Rhoda love him. He departs. He is killed. Susan marries a farmer ; Bernard marries, writes novels, and becomes more sociable and domesticated than ever ; Neville, fastidious and aloof, writes poetry, wins distinction, seeks privacy and perfection ; Jinny, the little animal, the rash, insatiable, gallant creature, loves and dances and enjoys her adventurous body, and faces old age with splendid fear and courage. Louis, driven by his inferiority complex, becomes a great business man ; but he preserves his attic room, where he and Rhoda, who have always felt themselves drawn together by their fears, their isolation (" for I am the weakest, the

youngest of them all," each thinks)—make love till
Rhoda leaves him. There is a final encounter of the
six in Hampton Court where they dine together ;
then Rhoda kills herself, and the others take their
destined way, and Bernard, an elderly man, sits sipping
brandy in a restaurant, summing up the story of their
lives.

We know, externally, very little about them. They
are the cultured, well-to-do characters common to
most of Mrs. Woolf's novels, but their external lives,
their relations to each other, are barely indicated.
Yet we know almost everything about them. For the
drama takes place not in the external world of speech
and action, but in the subconscious world, below
the articulate thoughts or spoken words with which
most novels are concerned. Down there, in the submarine cave of which Mrs. Woolf's characters are
always dreaming, moves the strange, subtle confusion
of memory, experience, contact and imagination
which forms the running stream below our surface
thoughts. It is a world hitherto largely neglected by
the English novelist. James Joyce, Dorothy Richardson, and D. H. Lawrence have adventured there ; but
their voyages of discovery have not been followed by
a general conquest. The territory is uncharted and
extremely hazardous, for only the most intent and
penetrating observation of human behaviour can make
a writer free of the unformed thoughts and impulses
of his characters. Yet these are as much a part of
" character " as their external acts, and it is with
character that the novelist is concerned. They are as

much a part of reality, and the extension of our knowledge of reality is his business. They inhabit a land where the law of reason does not run ; and Mrs. Woolf acknowledges allegiance to the law of reason. Yet in spite of these difficulties she has essayed the task, crossed the borders, and, finding the new land still sunk beneath a tossing sea, plunged bravely down to discover and reclaim.

The method that she has used to re-create this world is not entirely strange to her. Each character speaks in a kind of recitative, recording an individual current of subjective thought, somewhat after the fashion of *The Mark on the Wall*. These soliloquies are identified each only with the direction, " said Neville," " said Rhoda." Percival alone is seen only through the eyes of the Six. The others all reveal themselves and each other, personality, drama and development emerging slowly from the sequence of subconscious and conscious thought and memory. As in *To the Lighthouse*, maturity is bound to childhood by the influence of past desire. Rhoda, as a child at school, longs " to gather flowers and present them—oh, to whom ? " When she is a grown woman, and Percival whom she has loved is dead, she buys violets in Oxford Street and carries them to Greenwich, to scatter them to his memory on the river. Neville, as a little boy, overhears the cook talking, as she pulls out the dampers, about a man whose throat was cut ; and when he has grown up, and heard the news of Percival's death, this horror returns to him. " I will stand for one moment beneath the immitigable tree,

alone with the man whose throat is cut, while downstairs the cook shoves in and out the dampers. I will
not climb the stair. We are all doomed, all of us."
We forget nothing. Nothing is lost, nothing perishes.
The brass hoop still glitters on the cupboard ; the
ladies still sit between the long windows ; the children still scamper between the trees from Elvedon.
These memories are the ghosts that haunt us. While
we live, these endure.

And as the characters are bound to their own pasts,
so *The Waves* is bound in that strange unity which is
the artist's mind, to Mrs. Woolf's other novels. Susan,
thinking with satisfaction of her son, recalls that when
" the hinge of the gate is rusty, he heaves it open,"
and we are back on the road from Lincoln with Katharine Hilbery and William Rodney, when by heaving
open a rusty gate he won sufficient love from her to be
rejected. Susan's sons and daughters are " netted
over like fruit in their cots," like Mrs. Ramsay's
children. They play with skulls, like Jacob. An old,
unsteady woman with the bag trotting home under the
fire-red windows might be the old woman singing
outside the Union of London and Smiths Bank in
Jacob's Room ; she might be Mrs. McNab from *To the
Lighthouse.*

The relationships between the characters are conveyed with extraordinary subtlety, in a network of
reference. The affinity between Louis and Rhoda,
for instance, is suggested in the first chapter only by
Louis's observation that Rhoda does not run off with
the other four. So, at their last encounter, in Hampton

Court, she remains behind with him. He notices
her, too, alone in the schoolroom, where she has been
kept back to do her lessons. " And I, who speak
with an Australian accent, do not fear her as I fear the
others." Susan's love for Bernard is conveyed, never
from her own point of view, but from Louis's astringent
observation.

The method is confined to suggestion, reference,
repetition. The orchestral effect of several aspects
of consciousness playing together has been developed
from Mrs. Woolf's early experiments in *Monday
or Tuesday*. But here she acknowledges it. Bernard,
summing up the tale of the Six, says : " Neville, Susan,
Louis, Jinny, Rhoda and a thousand others, how
impossible to order them rightly ; to detach one
separately, or to give the effect of the whole—again
like music. What a symphony with its concord and
its discord, and its tunes on top and its complicated
bass beneath, then grew up ! Each played his own
tune, fiddle, flute, trumpet, drum or whatever the
instrument might be. With Neville, ' Let's discuss
Hamlet.' With Louis, science. With Jinny, love."
And because the instruments play tunes which run
below the surface of conscious thought, they need not
play in the idiom of the player. No little boy ever
thought in the words used by Louis as he stood hidden
in the thick wood before Jinny kissed him. " Flower
after flower is specked on the depths of green. The
petals are harlequins. Stalks rise from the black
hollows beneath. The flowers swim like fish made of
light upon the dark, green waters. I hold a stalk in

my hand. I am the stalk. My roots go down to the depths of the world, through earth dry with brick and damp earth, through veins of lead and silver. I am all fibre. All tremors shake me, and the weight of the earth is pressed to my ribs." That is no more the language of a little Australian boy standing lonely in an English garden than the opening passages of " The Prelude " represented Wordsworth's own phraseology in childhood ; but the sensations, the emotions are such as that little boy might have known. In translating them into words, Mrs. Woolf uses her own language. Her sentences keep their measured rhythm, and as one reads, one seems to hear beneath their melody, broken or sustained, beneath their formal phrases, such a surge and breathing of the sea as swings below the orchestration of Dame Ethel Smyth's, her friend's, opera, *The Wreckers*.

As its title suggests, it has been written under the spell of that sea-magic which affected the girl Virginia Stephen so profoundly. It is a novel of the sea ; yet all the events occur upon dry land. Interspersed between the episodes of the human story, it is true, she has set a series of pictures of the sea at dawn, in early morning, full daylight, noon, afternoon, sunset, evening, and night again, to correspond with the stages of human growth from childhood, through adolescence, youth and maturity to middle age, and the coming darkness of old age. The pictures are observed with glowing intensity of observation, and described in a type of poetical prose which Mrs. Woolf can write supremely well. Here, for instance, is a passage from Noon : " The sun, risen, no longer couched on a green mattress darting a fitful glance through watery jewels, bared its face and looked straight over the waves. They fell with a regular thud. They fell with the concussion of horses' hooves on the turf. Their spray rose like the tossing of lances and assegais over the riders' heads. They swept the beach with steel-blue and diamond-tipped water. They drew in and out with the energy, the muscularity, of an engine which sweeps its force out and in again."

These pictures have been seen, not from mid-ocean, but from a green and blossoming shore, set with gardens and woods and cornfields, in the centre of which stands a house—that house, presumably, in which the family of children did their lessons, that house, probably, from which Vanessa and Virginia Stephen were taken to be dipped in the Cornish sea.

The device is one familiar to poets. The impersonal, pictorial refrains of the old ballad form—

" All under a greenwood tree "

or

" The green leaves grow so bonny, oh ! "

or similar interpolations which set the human story against its background of rural scenery, have been used frequently with brilliant effect in traditional English poetry. But notably they have been used in ballads and folk songs ; all the world over, the irrelevant refrain is the mark of a simple, unsophisticated singing tradition—leaving a welcome pause in which the minstrel can collect his thoughts.

The question is how far this method can be successfully carried into a highly sophisticated, deliberate, and intellectually conceived work of literary prose. The pictures of the sea are in themselves beautiful. But I cannot feel sure that they were necessary. The waves were there in the book already, without being set in neatly framed seascapes and hung between each chapter.

They stir, rising and falling, through the whole design and rhythm of the book. That sea over which Rachel Vinrace sailed to Santa Marina, over which Tim Durrant and Jacob sailed to Cornwall, over which Cam and James and Mr. Ramsay sailed to the lighthouse, has now overflowed from its geographical significance. It has passed into time ; it has passed into the swing and surge of Mrs. Woolf's deliberate prose ; it has passed into the hearts and minds of men and women, until the characters themselves are tossed upon its restless waters, carried by the tide which is time to meet the final challenge of death. From cover to cover the novel is saturated in the sea. It dwells in the images that form themselves in the half-conscious thoughts of the six men and women with whom the story is concerned. When Neville rushes from the room at Cambridge, having flung his poem at Bernard, Bernard feels that " like a long wave, like a roll of heavy waters, he went over me, his devastating presence—dragging me open, laying bare the pebbles on the shore of my soul." Rhoda dreams that the petals rocking in her brown bowl are ships on the sea. Louis, as the farewell lunch to Percival ends, thinks how the temporary truce of feeling has been broken. " Now passions that lay in wait down there in the dark weeds which grow at the bottom rise and pound us with their waves." Even Jinny at the dance thinks, as her partner claims her, that she is like a limpet pulled from a rock. The sea spell, laid upon them in their childhood, binds them all.

This reiteration of sea-symbolism, this surge and rhythm of prose, these recurrent pictures of the sea, give an extraordinary effect of transparency and fluidity to the whole book, as though human life were already melted into a watery universe. Mrs. Dalloway's belief that after death she would become part of the house and trees, Betty Flanders' vision of Seabrook rolled round among rocks and stones, Mrs. Ramsay's personality, after her death, mingling with the earth and air and thoughts of her friends ; all this Wordsworthian conception of the unity of human and non-human life has here been developed into a new medium for revelation—for that extension of our understanding of reality which Mrs. Woolf demands of art. Hitherto she has laid her symbolism within action ; Rachel Vinrace sailed out on the voyage of life's adventure ; Mrs. Ramsay was the light of the lighthouse which she saw. But now she both places her symbolism outside, in the objective sea-pictures, quite unrelated to the history of her characters, and at the same time draws all life as though through a submarine vision. Time, words, loves, ambitions and the changing souls and bodies of men drift down the stream of Heracleitan flux : " παντα ρέι "—all things flow, rocking together in the ocean of sub-conscious thought.

And the universe has been stripped like a bather for its submergence. The cinematograph show of outward pose and gesture moving so vividly through *Jacob's Room* has gone. Here the characters are seen without their trappings of flesh and bone, surnames, positions and continuous narrative. They have been flayed, uncovered. They move through their history of growth, fixture and decay like naked bathers under water, so that at first it is not easy for the reader to discern what they are doing, any more than it is easy, while floating on the blue waters of the Mediterranean, to see the fishes, weeds and stones and wreckage at the bottom. But if we can slide like fish below the surface ; if we can discipline our eyes to keep wide open there, gazing downward at the sandy floor beneath us, we can behold a world of hidden beauty, well worth the pain of stinging eyeballs.

The writing is extraordinarily rich in texture. That is why it will bear reading and re-reading, for each time the reader lets down his net into Mrs. Woolf's *Waves* he will bring it up heavy with live, sparkling fishes of thought and observation. " Rhoda came wandering vaguely. . . . What fear wavered and hid itself and blew to a flame in the depths of her grey, her startled, her dreaming eyes ? Cruel and vindictive as we are, we are not bad to that extent. We have our fundamental goodness surely, or to talk as I talk freely to someone I hardly know would be impossible—we should cease." " But if you hold a blunt blade to a grindstone long enough, something spurts—a jagged edge of fire ; so held to lack of reason, aimlessness, the usual, all massed together, out spurted in one flame hatred, contempt." " And being in love for the first time, I made a phrase—a poem about a wood pigeon—a single phrase, for a hole had been knocked in my mind, one of those sudden transparencies through which one sees everything."

It is all alive and yet compressed, packed, rich, full, fertile. Mrs. Woolf's thought has not been cramped but enriched by achieving expression through six different personalities. The advice which she gives to her young friend in her *Letter to a Young Poet* she has here herself practised. " The art of writing," she told him, " . . . can be learned . . . much more drastically and effectively by imagining that one is not oneself but somebody different." Hamlet, Falstaff and Cleopatra, she says, taught Shakespeare how to write. The aggressive Louis, the sensuous Jinny, the fell, possessive, passionate Susan, the loquacious, sociable Bernard, have taught Mrs. Woolf how to write *The Waves*.

The beauty, the profundity, the technical accomplishment of the book are great. Mrs. Woolf has achieved in it the music and subtlety of poetry. Like poetry, its reading demands disciplined attention ; but its prose deprives us of that lilt, that swing of words, which carry us through a long and difficult poem. Yet if we listen and wait for it, in all moments of excitement, the rhythm comes, the same rhythm as that which stirred in Mrs. Woolf's affirmation of life at the

end of *An Unwritten Novel*. Perhaps it is true that in
all moments of high emotional tension each great prose-
writer has a particular rhythm, a cadence, to which his
words naturally turn. For as, twelve years before,
the adventure of Minnie Marsh closed on a song of
glory in praise of life, so does Bernard's soliloquy,
which sums up *The Waves*, close on a song of glory
in defiance of death. The words, the occasion, the
sentiment are different ; but the cadence and spirit
of the writer have not changed.

The earlier passage ends : ". . . Grey is the landscape, dim as ashes ; the water murmurs and moves.
If I fall on my knees, if I go through the ritual, the
ancient antics, it's you, unknown figures, you I adore ;
if I open my arms, it's you I embrace, you I draw to
me—adorable world ! "

Here is the conclusion to *The Waves* :

" And in me too the wave rises. It swells ; it
arches its back. I am aware once more of a new desire,
something rising beneath me like the proud horse
whose rider first spurs and then pulls him back. What
enemy do we now perceive advancing against us, you
whom I ride now, as we stand pawing this stretch of
pavement ? It is death. Death is the enemy. It is
death against whom I ride with my spear couched
and my hair flying back like a young man's, like
Percival's when he galloped in India. I strike spurs
into my horse. Against you I will fling myself,
unvanquished and unyielding, O Death !

" The waves broke on the shore."

The conclusion is characteristic. It is an affirmation

199

of life. Death is the enemy ; death, not only of the body, but of the mind, the perceptive spirit, the faculty by which man recognises truth. In *Night and Day*, in *Mrs. Dalloway* and *To the Lighthouse*, the same note was sounded. Mrs. Woolf's vindication of life is not praise of the blind animal " Life-Force." She is not a vitalist. For her to have life, and to have it more abundantly, means to have ever intenser faculties of perception and understanding.

It is in her intellectual position rather than her methods and technique that she stands apart from Joyce, and, I think, from Proust. Her vision is intensely individual ; but her philosophy is not wholly individualistic. She acknowledges tradition ; she acknowledges discipline ; she acknowledges the unifying power of common conviction and experience ; she accepts the driving mastery of the idea.

About her future work, prophecy is dangerous. One of the most interesting qualities of her mind is its elasticity. The two streams of thought—one practical, controversial, analytical ; the other creative, poetical, audacious—may continue to run separately, or they may flow together again as in her first two novels.

We cannot predict what problem will attract, what beauty entrance her next ; but there are certain things that it seems probable she cannot and will not do : violence, farce, the humour of eccentricity, mastered by Scott in his peasants and by Dickens in his Cockneys, are beyond her. The immense detailed knowledge of the material circumstances of life mastered by Thackeray or Arnold Bennett is beyond her. She will remain—it seems possible—shut off from intimate contact with Hilda Thomas of Putney and Edgar J. Watkiss, who lays lead piping among the bowels of Bond Street. She may catch a fleeting vision of their world. Moggridge may sit for a moment opposite Minnie Marsh at Eastbourne ; Mrs. McNab may decide that she could do no harm in picking the Ramsays' flowers—and, indeed, these glimpses of insight into the minds of Mrs. McNab and Minnie Marsh may be among her surest, her most successful flashes of intuition. But they are glimpses only. The intimate and prolonged knowledge necessary for a complete revelation of such characters is not here. It seems only too true that hardly more than once in five hundred years is an artist born who unites extreme subtlety of mind with wide experience of living—a Shakespeare or a Tolstoi.

We may, perhaps, prophesy that her range will remain limited, her contact with life delicate and profound rather than comprehensive ; that her novels will grow more subtle and intricate as her criticism grows more orderly, stiffened perhaps into some kind of system. It is possible, since her talent evidently flowered late and is still developing, that she will continue to grow in breadth and power as she grows in wisdom. But she is unlikely ever to command the allegiance of a wide contemporary public. It is possible that the changing shape of the novel may make her obscurities clear and her strangeness familiar, so that her circle of readers will widen rather than narrow with the passing years. But at present there is still only a minority which prefers *To the Lighthouse*, with its demands upon the reader's intelligence and imagination, to a novel such as *The Good Companions*, which tells a pleasant, full and easy tale.

Yet she has qualities which will wear better than mere readability or the luxury of romance. Her art is tragic. She understands all shades of grief ; life passes before her under the perpetual menace of death, which robs even while it fulfils. For all her lightness of touch, her moth-wing humour, her capricious irrelevance, she writes as one who has looked upon the worst that life can do to man and woman, upon every sensation of loss, bewilderment and humiliation ; and yet the corroding acid of disgust has not defiled her. She is in love with life. It is this quality which lifts her beyond the despairs and fashions of her age, which gives to her vision of reality a radiance, a wonder, unshared by any other living writer. She has, one feels, seen everything and remained undaunted, understood all fear and all humiliation and, accepting it, declared that life was good. It is this which places her work, meagre though its amount may hitherto have been, slight in texture and limited in scope, beside the work of the great masters. A largeness of conception, a majestic curiosity, an all-embracing love for the complexities and contradictions of the universe, and an integrity of spirit in the pursuit of truth do not appear in little minds. In spite of her isolation, her fragility, her limited experience, any chance figure casually seen in the street, any word, any contact is capable of stirring her to that excitement

of the imagination which is the first condition of
creative art.

" And yet the last look of them—he stepping from
the kerb and she following him round the edge of the
big building—brims me with wonder, floods me anew.
Mysterious figures ! Mother and son, who are you ?
Why do you walk down the street ? Where to-night
will you sleep, and then, to-morrow ? . . . I start
after them. People drive this way and that. The
white light splutters and pours. . . . I hasten, I follow.
This, I fancy, must be the sea. Grey is the landscape,
dim as ashes ; the water murmurs and moves. If
I fall on my knees, if I go through the ritual, the
ancient antics, it's you, unknown figures, you I adore ;
if I open my arms, it's you I embrace, you I draw to
me—adorable world ! "

BIBLIOGRAPHY

Date.	Title and Description.	Publisher.
1915	THE VOYAGE OUT. (Novel.)	*Duckworth & Co.*
1917	TWO STORIES. (In collaboration with Leonard Woolf.)	*Hogarth Press*
1919	NIGHT AND DAY. (Novel.)	*Duckworth & Co.*
	KEW GARDENS. (Sketch.)	*Hogarth Press*
	THE MARK ON THE WALL. (Sketch.)	*Hogarth Press*
1921	MONDAY OR TUESDAY. (Collection of Sketches.)	*Hogarth Press*
1922	JACOB'S ROOM. (Novel.)	*Hogarth Press*
	" Stavrogin's Confession." (Three hitherto unpublished chapters of Dostoevsky's novel, " The Possessed," and " The Plan of the Life of a Great Sinner." Translated into English by S. S. Koteliansky and Virginia Woolf.)	*Hogarth Press*
1923	TOLSTOI'S LOVE LETTERS. (With a study of the autobiographical elements in Tolstoi's work, by Paul Biryukov. Translated by S. S. Koteliansky and Virginia Woolf.)	*Hogarth Press*
	TALKS WITH TOLSTOI. (By A. B. Goldenveizer. Translated by S. S. Koteliansky and Virginia Woolf.)	*Hogarth Press*
1924	MR. BENNETT AND MRS. BROWN. (Critical Essay.)	*Hogarth Press*

Date.	Title and Description.	Publisher.
1925	MRS. DALLOWAY. (Novel.)	Hogarth Press
	THE COMMON READER. (Collected Critical Essays.)	Hogarth Press
1926	Introduction to "Victorian Photographs," by Julia M. Cameron.	Hogarth Press
1927	TO THE LIGHTHOUSE. (Novel.)	Hogarth Press
1928	Introduction to Sterne's "Sentimental Journey." (World's Classics Series.)	Oxford University Press
	ORLANDO. A BIOGRAPHY. (Fantasy.)	Hogarth Press
1929	A ROOM OF ONE'S OWN. (Essay.)	Hogarth Press
1930	ON BEING ILL. (Essay.)	Hogarth Press
	BEAU BRUMMEL.	(Published in U.S.A.)
1931	Introduction to "Life as We have Known it." (Biographical Sketches by Women of the Co-operative Guild.)	Hogarth Press
	THE WAVES. (Novel.)	
1932	A LETTER TO A YOUNG POET. (Essay.)	Hogarth Press

Note.—A large number of Mrs. Woolf's critical articles and sketches are still uncollected, and can only be found in back files of *The Times Literary Supplement, The Nation and Athenæum, The Athenæum, Vogue, Time and Tide, The London Mercury, The New York Herald Tribune, The New Republic* (U.S.A.), *Criterion, Life and Letters, Saturday Review of Literature* (U.S.A.), *Atlantic Monthly* (U.S.A.), *Bookman* (U.S.A.), *Yale Review* (U.S.A.).

By far the fullest study of Mrs. Woolf's work hitherto printed is *Le Roman psychologique de Virginia Woolf*, by Florio Delattre. Published by J. Vrin. Paris. 1932.

Printed in England at THE BALLANTYNE PRESS
SPOTTISWOODE, BALLANTYNE & CO. LTD.
Colchester, London & Eton